CALIFORNIA

Land and Legacy

A Project of the Conservation Fund

William Fulton

Foreword by **Kevin Starr**

WESTCLIFFE PUBLISHERS

PREFACE

California is like no other place on earth. It is constantly changing and evolving, and as each new epoch emerges, California faces—and usually meets—a new set of challenges.

This book resulted from a series of conversations about the future of California with my brother, Bill Lane, former publisher of *Sunset* magazine; William Reilly, the former administrator of the U.S. Environmental Protection Agency; Doug Wheeler, Secretary of the Resources Agency of California; Pat Noonan of The Conservation Fund; and Henry Diamond of Beveridge & Diamond, P.C. As we contemplated the 150th anniversary of this remarkable place, it became apparent that yet another epoch is emerging here, presenting us with a new set of challenges. The population continues to grow. The economic structure continues to evolve. And the state's demographic makeup is changing more rapidly than at any time in the last century.

All these trends mean that the task of conserving the state's spectacular land and natural resources is more urgent than ever. Just as surely, however, it is clear that the formula for success in this endeavor will be very different in the future than it has been in the past.

Three decades ago—or even two—conservation was viewed as a government task, to be undertaken by resource scientists at public agencies armed with sufficient funding to get the job done. Today, it is clear that the task of conservation belongs to all of us. The political will and resources required to meet the conservation challenge must emerge from a broad range of efforts—not just the government, but also private individuals and corporations, as well as non-profit organizations and other institutions—all working together toward a common set of goals.

California has been at the forefront of this trend. In recent years, for example, California has created two important models for consensus-oriented regional conservation planning. The first is CALFED, the collaborative state-federal effort to restore the ecological health of the Sacramento-San Joaquin Delta. The second is the Natural Communities Conservation Planning program, which has led to the creation of eleven sub-regional conservation plans in Southern California. These models show how government agencies can work together—and with private and non-profit sectors—in creating a broad-ranging yet workable regional framework for conservation efforts.

Mountain dogwood in autumn color amid giant sequoia trees, Sequoia National Park

Larry Ulrich

Just as important, California has been a leader in developing innovative implementation tools to make sure the job gets done "on the ground." And it is here that government collaboration with other sectors has proven to be important. Both for-profit and non-profit organizations have thrived in creating and operating "mitigation banks," which permit the conservation of large swaths of property. Similarly, buying and selling water rights is beginning to emerge as a major conservation tool, allowing water to be used for environmental purposes while encouraging water conservation in both agricultural and urban water systems. As these two examples suggest, the future of conservation in California is clearly transactional in nature—creating viable markets that bring buyers and sellers together in a way that achieves overall conservation goals.

In the finest tradition of California entrepreneurship, these planning and implementation approaches have helped to nurture a whole new industry into existence. This emerging industry includes private landowners who hold themselves to a high standard of land stewardship, philanthropic institutions focused on conservation, and a cadre of thriving land trusts and other non-profit groups. It also includes a new generation of consumers who value not only the qualities of nature but also its relationship to places and communities. Together these forces are promoting more sustainable patterns of development.

This is the beginning of a remarkable achievement, but it is not yet complete. Even with all the promising trends described above, this new approach to California conservation is still in its infancy. True, many of the necessary partnerships and tools have been put into place, but they are not yet in widespread use. As the next epoch unfolds, we will have a rare opportunity to reinvent the whole idea of conservation in California— and, in the process, achieve far more than we could have accomplished the old way.

Meeting this challenge will require a major commitment by the people of California—as well as by the government, private, and non-profit organizations devoted to conservation. It will, as described above, require innovative partnerships that cross traditional boundaries both bureaucratic and geographic. And it will require proactive planning, permitting some quality development in appropriate areas, yet still allowing us to "get ahead of the curve" so that we no longer face the extinction of species and the destruction of precious resources as everyday events. Perhaps most important, it will require that California's human capital be brought to bear on the problem.

Yosemite Valley was one of the first of California's natural wonders to be preserved. Many more remain at risk.

Through a century and a half of change and evolution, California has remained a truly extraordinary place—a place where people can achieve their full potential and still maintain a close relationship to the natural environment. I believe that if we take bold action now, California can remain a special place for the next century and a half—and beyond.

—MELVIN B. LANE
Menlo Park, California
June 1998

ACKNOWLEDGMENTS

Many individuals and institutions contributed valuable time and resources to the development and creation of *California: Land and Legacy*. The Conservation Fund wishes to recognize, in particular, three individuals who have made outstanding contributions not just to this book but also to conservation in California.

Laurence William Lane, Jr., A.O., first envisioned this book and later provided his experience and support to make it a reality. Former publisher of *Sunset* magazine and co-chairman of Lane Publishing Co., Bill has served in presidential administrations on diplomatic, environmental, and national park matters, often involving land and water conservation in the West. He has served as ambassador to Australia and ambassador-at-large in Japan. Bill's commitment to the environment started in his youth, when he worked as a guide and packer in Sequoia and Yosemite National Parks during the Depression. Through the years, he has gone on to receive numerous awards from environmental and conservation organizations for his effective and dedicated service.

Melvin B. Lane has made significant contributions to environmental protection in California in both professional and personal capacities. Former president and co-chairman of Lane Publishing Co., Mel has also served on the boards of international, national, and local conservation organizations and commissions. Perhaps his greatest contributions have been to shoreline preservation, which began with his appointment as chairman of the San Francisco Bay Conservation and Development Commission and continued when he was named the first chairman of the California Coastal Commission.

Richard N. Goldman, chairman and former chief executive officer of Richard N. Goldman & Co., serves as president for both the Goldman Environmental Foundation and The Richard and Rhoda Goldman Fund. Mr. Goldman has given generously to the arts and to environmental causes, but is perhaps best known for establishing the Goldman Environmental Prize. Awarded by the Goldman Environmental Foundation, this prize is considered the Nobel prize for the environment because of the prestige it carries in honoring grass-roots environmentalists throughout the world.

The Conservation Fund also extends its gratitude to those individuals who gave significantly of their time to make this book possible: Michael A. Mantell of the California Environmental Trust and Beveridge & Diamond, P.C.; Henry L. Diamond of Beveridge & Diamond, P.C.; Douglas P. Wheeler, Secretary for the Resources Agency of California; and William K. Reilly, former administrator of the U.S. Environmental Protection Agency. All contributed invaluable advice. Patrick Noonan provided vision, leadership, and guidance. Sydney Macy and Anne Gore worked behind the scenes in many different capacities. Douglas Horne expertly managed the project from start to finish with characteristic enthusiasm, ingenuity, and excellence.

Special thanks are also due to The Ambassador Bill & Jean Lane Fund at The Peninsula Community Foundation; The Richard & Rhoda Goldman Fund; The James Irvine Foundation; and The Jackson Hole Preserve, Incorporated, and its chairman, Clayton W. Frye, Jr., for their generous support of this publication and their enduring commitment to conservation.

Salt flats reflect distant mountain ridges, Death Valley National Park

Charles Gurche

Seeking Solutions:
The Conservation Fund

The Conservation Fund is a national, non-profit organization that seeks sustainable conservation solutions for the twenty-first century by emphasizing the integration of economic and environmental goals. Through real estate transactions, demonstration projects, education, and community outreach activities, the Fund designs innovative long-term measures to conserve land and water resources. Since its inception in 1985, the Fund has forged partnerships to protect more than 1.5 million acres of America's land legacy.

Western dogwood blossoms brighten a redwood forest, Sequoia National Forest

Jack Dykinga

INTERNATIONAL STANDARD BOOK NUMBER:
1-56579-281-5

EDITOR: Suzanne Venino
DESIGNER: Rebecca Finkel, F + P Graphic Design
PRODUCTION MANAGER: Harlene Finn

TEXT:
© 1998 William Fulton. ALL RIGHTS RESERVED.

PUBLISHER'S CATALOGING-IN-PUBLICATION
Fulton, William B., 1955–
    California: land and legacy / text by
William Fulton ; a project of the
Conservation Fund. — 1st ed.
    p. cm.
    Includes bibliographical references.
    ISBN: 1-56579-281-5

    1. Land use—California—History.
2. Landscape changes—California—
History. 3. Human geography—
California—History. 4. California—
History. I. Conservation Fund
(Arlington, Va.) II. Title

GF504.C2F85 1998   333.73'09794
                         QBI98-772

PUBLISHER:
Westcliffe Publishers, Inc.
P.O. Box 1261
Englewood, Colorado 80150

PRINTED IN HONG KONG
BY C & C OFFSET PRINTING CO., LTD.

For more information about other fine books
and calendars from Westcliffe Publishers,
please call your local bookstore, contact us
1-800-523-3692, or write for our free catalog.

PHOTO ON PAGE *1*:
Leafing oaks in spring, Mendocino National Forest,
by John Fielder

A NOTE ABOUT SOURCES

Writing this book required me to consult hundreds of sources, including books, articles, and doctoral dissertations, as well as make a series of field visits to different locations around the state. Simply listing all the sources would fill an entire book in itself, and I have tried to give credit in the text to authors whose work especially assisted me. But a few particular sources stand out, and I would like to mention those here.

I consulted most of the standard histories of California, but especially useful were *California: An Interpretive History,* by James J. Rawls and Walton Bean, and *The Elusive Eden,* by Richard B. Rice, William A. Bullough, and Richard J. Orsi, which focuses on the environment and natural resources. The classic nineteenth-century histories of California by Hubert Howe Bancroft and Theodore H. Hittell were wonderful resources, as was another classic, William Brewer's *Up and Down California, 1860–1864*.

By far the best technical source I consulted was *An Island Called California* by Elna Bakker, a delightfully accessible tour of the state's natural communities. Carey McWilliams's *California: The Great Exception,* published at the time of the state's centennial in 1950, is peerless in its ability to paint California's first century in broad strokes. *California Lands: Ownership, Use, and Management,* published by the American Forestry Association in 1958, was a vital source of information. *Gold v. Grain: The Mining Debris Controversy* by Robert L. Kelley is still authoritative some forty years after its original publication. *Energy And the Making of Modern California* by James C. Williams and *An Ocean of Oil* by Robert Sollen provided insight into specific resources, as did Michael Williams's *Americans and Their Forests: A Historical Geography,* which has an excellent section on West Coast logging and California in particular.

Norris Hundley's *The Great Thirst* is the best book ever written about water in California. *The Last Stand: The War Between Wall Street and Main Street Over California's Redwoods,* by David Harris, is a vivid account. *The Great California Deserts* by W. Storrs Lee is wonderful story-telling, and *The Mojave: A Portrait of the Definitive American Desert* by David Darlington is great journalism.

To these and all the other sources I consulted, I give my gratitude, though any errors, of course, belong to me alone.

—W.F.

Jerry Sieve

Massive trunks of giant sequoias, Grant's Grove area of Sequoia National Park

Table of Contents

Foreword

Foreword

Giant sequoias,
Sequoia National Park

William Neill

In this remarkable book, at once lavish and succinct, noted planning expert William Fulton has chronicled the history of California from an environmental perspective. In the long run, this history—California as land and sea, as air and water, as minerals, flora, and fauna—is the most important history of all, for without the continuing vitality of California as a physical place, the human story and the human future would soon cease.

Had this book been written two or three decades ago, it might have assumed a more apocalyptic tone, as did so many environmental writings of that era. It was at this point, after all, just around the time of the Santa Barbara oil spill of 1969, that environmentalists awoke—with a shuddering shock—to just how much had been used up, squandered, and wasted in the creation of California as a human community. From that awareness came a counterassault by conservationists that, while not ending the destruction entirely, dramatically held it in check. It was an emergency situation, and as in the case of all emergencies, there was little time for subtlety and balanced equations.

As this historical survey of the California environment suggests, a new and more subtle plateau is being achieved in reviewing our stewardship of California. The Conservation Fund, forever improvising to find conservation solutions that work in time and place, challenged Fulton to identify the ideas and ideals that have spurred Californians to move dramatically through their landscape. The result is a book whose power—aside from its comprehensiveness, its precision and balance—is in its acceptance, indeed respect, for the inevitability of the human factor. From this perspective, *California: Land and Legacy* ranks as a general history of California. Its point of view, of course, is upon the environmental effects of human action, but the human factor is essential to its story. It is the story of both land and people.

In the first phase of corrective environmental writing—the shocked phase, if you will, the apocalyptic phase of thirty years ago—so many environmental writers, in chronicling their woeful story of misuse, hovered on the very edge of suggesting that perhaps it would have been better for California, as a human society, never to have happened at all, or at least never to have happened beyond the Native American era. This survey, by contrast, while never flinching from the devastating effects of human misuse, is nevertheless based upon the assumption that California has been, and will continue to be, an inevitable interaction between human beings and the environment.

Most deeply and fundamentally, William Fulton is by profession and instinct a planner; and planners, by their very definition, believe in some kind of future, or what is there to plan for? Planners also know their history, as does Fulton. Indeed, he reads the landscapes, seascapes, and skyscapes of California, its climate eco-zones, its preserved and its squandered spaces, its successful and unsuccessful settlements, as if California as place, as environment, were one vast historical text, which it is.

California: Land and Legacy reads, decodes, and interprets the present-tense environment of California as a distillation of past, present, and future. The Gold Rush, with its terrible legacy of hydraulic mining; the use of Gold Rush technology—the movement of land and water—to create an infrastructure of agriculture and irrigation; and the further refinement of that technology—moving water across the land and delivering it to precise places—to metropolitanize the state at the beginning of this century; the post-war rise of population from nine million to twenty-two million in twenty swift years, with its concomitant construction of suburbs and freeways: again and again this book underscores the transformations and, even more, the transformations within transformations that are part and parcel of the history of California. The story of human settlement and its interaction with the environment, whether for good or for evil or a mixture of both, shifts and re-shifts like windblown dunes on the desert, like ever-changing cloud formations overhead, like surf breaking and re-breaking along the 1,100 miles of the California Coast.

In this story of transformation, moreover, can be found the paradigms for a better or a worse future. Such paradigms can only be found here, in fact, for in environmental terms, California has only this history, this one environmental legacy. In terms of the past and the present, there is no other possible scenario. In terms of the future, however, there remains an open question.

Will we learn from the past? Even more basically, *can* we learn from the past? Can we at once bring together the peoples of the world, including the dispossessed eager for upward mobility, hence for the utilization of resources, and still fashion a properly balanced and effective conservation program? No amount of wishful thinking can banish the challenge of future growth. California will grow by ten, even fifteen million people within the next few decades. This is inevitable. Some demographers predict a population of sixty-two million by 2040.

Even if such predicted growth were reduced by one half, it would be challenge enough. Thirty years ago, Californians became overwhelmingly aware of how much had been lost. Today, if William Fulton's book is any indication, we are aware, simultaneously, of what has been lost, what has been properly used, and what awaits our proper and improper action in the years to come. The apocalyptic mode of the 1960s yields to a more mature sense—a true conservationist's sense—of tragedy and possibility, correct stewardship in the face of inevitable growth, or squandering, shortsighted decisions. For those who align themselves, defiantly, on the side of optimism, this accurate and reasonable historical inventory of California as place on Planet Earth offers a steady, understated, but persistent chord of hope.

—KEVIN STARR
State Librarian of California

The California Attitude

One hundred and fifty years ago, the Golden Gate was a spectacular natural land formation—visible to passing sailors, unconnected by any handsome bridges of human creation, serving as the entrance to one of the greatest natural estuaries in the world. San Francisco was a town of two thousand people, typically rowdy but barely intruding on the pristine and treeless peninsula on which it was located. The vast Central Valley produced no food—at least not the kind of cultivated food that people all over the world put on their table every day—yet its multitude of rivers and wetlands supported a diversity of fish and wildlife unmatched anywhere else. The forests of the North Coast were almost untouched, producing, as they had for hundreds of years, some of the largest and most magnificent trees in creation. Southern California was a dusty, semi-arid land dotted with a few Roman Catholic missions that grew irrigated crops with the help of what remained of once-thriving tribes of Native Americans. Almost seven decades after its founding, Los Angeles remained quite literally a "cowtown," deriving most of its wealth from cowhides and candle tallow made from cow fat. And underneath the flowing rivers and plentiful oak woodlands of the Sierra Nevada lay an unknown, untapped lode of the world's most precious metal.

Then the sluice gates opened and down out of the Sierra Foothills poured gold. And not just a little gold, but such vast amounts of gold that it transformed California almost instantaneously into a modern society. Two years after gold was first discovered near a sawmill on the South Fork of the American River in 1848, California was delivering $10 million a year of the precious metal to the rest of the world. Two years after that, the figure had risen to $80 million, and California was producing most of the world's gold. As news of the gold strike spread, a staggering number of people arrived in search of their fortune. From a non-Indian population of only a few thousand at the time of the discovery, California grew to 20,000 people the first year, 100,000 the second, and 200,000 by 1852, just four years after gold was first

Lichen-covered granite boulders in open oak woodlands, Sequoia National Park

Fred Hirschmann

discovered. This great influx of humanity came from all over the world—from the East Coast, Hawaii, China, Ireland, and Germany—enhancing California's well-established status as a multi-cultural society.

But as the great California writer Carey McWilliams observed a half-century ago, the actual discovery and production of gold was probably the least important aspect of the entire story. Far more important was the fact that gold gave California an immediate base of wealth unmatched in American history, and the Gold Rush quickly created a vast and affluent market for practically everything. More than one historian has pointed out that California benefited far more from the merchants and capitalists who fleeced the miners of their gold than from actually mining the golden fleece.

Within two years of the discovery at Sutter's Mill, gold gave California such political power that it leapfrogged over half the country to become a state. Within five years, it had generated such wealth that capitalists set up large-scale mining operations and began to squeeze out the little guys with their sluice boxes. And within a decade, gold had made San Francisco into one of the nation's leading cities, jump-starting its transformation into the only city west of St. Louis capable of financing the growth and development of the American frontier.

In other words, gold allowed California to simply bypass the long, slow process of agrarian development that other states had taken many decades to pass through. It generated the vast wealth required to unlock the massive potential of a tough but fragile region. Gold formed the basis for virtually every other aspect of California's early development. It hastened the exploration of the redwood forests and created a huge market for lumber products in San Francisco, thus stimulating the state's massive timber industry. It laid the foundation for California's vast agricultural industry by populating the Central Valley with thousands of would-be miners who saw farming as a more attractive long-term career. It even set the stage for the large-scale urban development of the twentieth century by forcing the rapid creation of a sophisticated system for settling competing claims to large tracts of land.

Most important, gold gave California a worldwide cache as a glamorous and exciting place where anything was possible. Little wonder that while other states adopted mottos like "Live Free or Die" and "Ever Upward," California's motto has always been "I Have Found It" ("Eureka")—the "it" meaning not only gold, but just about any limitless goal of human activity that seemed impossible to achieve anywhere else. "In California," Carey McWilliams wrote at the time of state's centennial in 1950, "the lights went on all at once, in a blaze, and they have never dimmed."

California has aptly been described as an island, sealed off from the rest of the world by deserts, mountains, and the Pacific Ocean. So complete is California's physical separation that—like Australia—it is a kind of self-contained biological experiment, full of plant and animal species found nowhere else in the world. California, according to Elna Bakker, a leading chronicler of California's natural communities, "has developed in its own way and at its own pace; evolutionary history here has woven numerous distinctive patterns of interaction between life form and the land." As a result, Bakker adds: "Lichen-shrouded sea-mist forest is but an hour's drive from a mineral-encrusted dry lake. Prairie and the world's tallest forest are only a few feet apart." California's patterns "have similarities, but no exact duplicates elsewhere in the world." They are "incredibly intricate, multiple, and unfortunately irreplaceable."

After the Gold Rush, however, the explosive nature of the state's development quickly turned the island into a hothouse. Modern California was such a magnetic locale, formed so quickly and with such blistering intensity, that it fired the creation of a wholly different way of looking at the world—a viewpoint that can only be called "the California attitude."

Maybe the most basic component of the California attitude is the comfortable, almost casual, manner in which Californians take the relentless velocity of their society in stride. Given the state's history, this nonchalance shouldn't be surprising. From the Gold Rush onward, the state's wealth and growth have occurred at warp speed. And so Californians are accustomed to operating in a fast-moving environment where change itself is the only constant.

But the underlying terrain across which Californians move so quickly is a vast and magnificent canvas. Like most of the American West, California is at once dramatic and fragile. It is awe-inspiring in its scale and potential, and the variety of its natural resources is breathtaking—ranging from stark, rugged mountains to fertile valleys to unparalleled coastline. Yet California's resources are hard to crack open and easily damaged once the tampering begins. California's natural wonders have often left even its most ruthless developers speechless with awe. "Almost the first thought passing in one's mind, as he enters a virgin forest of redwoods," wrote journalist and businessman Charles Goodwin Noyes in 1884, "is one of pity that such a wonderful creation of nature should be subject to the greed of man for gold." So rapt was Noyes by nature that he included these words in a book prepared especially to interest Eastern capitalists in investing in the California redwood industry.

This rare combination of velocity and scale means that Californians have always had an intense relationship with the landscape. By skipping over the agrarian phase of development, California also skipped the slow and agonizing process of taming the landscape—farm by farm, tree by tree, stump by stump—that characterized the rest of the nation. And so many parts of the state remain raw and wild. Even today, a new subdivision almost anywhere in the state is likely to intrude on an untamed landscape never before disturbed by humans.

Thus, any collision between a Californian and the state's natural resources is likely to be a jarring one. And over the past century and a half, Californians have developed a distinct taste for these jarring collisions with nature and have sought to experience nature in a way that is at once wild and civilized—to ride it and tame it both at the same time.

Today, we see this attitude play out every day on the waves and in the mountains through such distinctively California pastimes as surfing and mountain biking. These pastimes seek out an "in-your-face" encounter with nature, but they also try to soften and manage the experience with such modern inventions as wet suits and shock absorbers. A century before the invention of the wet suit, however, this jarring collision with nature—the manipulation of a resource with unprecedented speed and force—was already present in the California attitude.

When panning for gold no longer yielded results and digging for gold proved too difficult, enterprising Californians in the 1850s came up with a better idea. They discovered that they could save days of effort simply by hosing down the gravel hillsides of Nevada County with vast quantities of water—washing the mountains away and leaving the gold behind. Before long, "hydraulic mining" had become a capital-intensive business, producing large quantities of wealth with great efficiency by creating a jarring collision between Californians and nature.

It was the first of many capital-intensive, large-scale methods that Californians used to unlock the great potential that nature held for them. Though the process was extractive, the effect was also miraculously transformative. Everywhere else in the West, the mining of precious metals created a boom-and-bust economy controlled by absentee owners. In California it created indigenous wealth that stimulated cycle after cycle of transformation.

These transformations have taken many forms. Sometimes, they have been transformations of nature that helped build modern California—aqueducts, vast farms, railroads, and highways. Other times, the result has been a chain reaction of events unprecedented in human history. The Gold Rush, for example, helped create a powerful railroad, which in turn generated the wealth that allowed Leland Stanford to endow a great university, which in turn spawned the growth of Silicon Valley, which changed the world in a thousand different ways and brought more wealth back to California, to be recycled yet again—a millennium of change in only 150 years.

The message contained in such examples is clear: Over and over again, that jarring collision between Californians and nature has transformed California from a myth into a reality far beyond anything the myth could have promised. And in the process, it has reaffirmed the belief of most Californians in transformation as the foundation of their identity. After a century and a half in the hothouse, Californians believe they do not extract; they do not reinvent; they do not alter; they *transform.* They take what they have been given, manipulate it on a grand scale, and create something entirely new in the process.

California has paid a big price for this transformation, however. Jarring collisions with nature may be exhilarating—and profitable—but they are not always good for nature. And, ironically, very often they turn out to be bad for people too, at least in the long run. California's history, and its present-day landscape, are quite literally littered with testaments to this relentless equation.

Hydraulic mining, for example, turned out to be a threat to the very people who profited from it. The Sacramento Valley town of Marysville grew prosperous manufacturing the artillery-style "monitors" that were used to hammer the hillsides with water. It wasn't long, however, before the debris shaken lose by this artillery came barreling back down the Feather River, threatening the existence of the town where the equipment that dislodged the debris was made.

Nor is that the end of the story. More than a century after hydraulic mining was halted in California, the debris is still flowing down the Feather and Sacramento Rivers, raising the water level significantly. Marysville still must protect itself with levees that wall the town off from the outside world. Sacramento, now a metropolis of a million people, is the most flood-prone large city in America. And landowners up and down the Sacramento Valley are still suing each other over who should be responsible.

When hydraulic mining finally was halted, it wasn't because of the environmental devastation the process wreaked. It was because the rising waters of the Feather and Sacramento Rivers threatened another great transforming manipulation of nature—the cultivation of the Central Valley. As we shall see, the agriculture industry had its own sweeping effect on California's growth. And it has created its own environmental backlash by depriving the Sacramento Delta of the flushes of freshwater needed for wildlife to survive there. Just as an explosive chain of events has led from the Gold Rush to modern-day Silicon Valley, so too have chain reactions of environmental side-effects built upon one another in California until they have reached monumental proportions.

Thus, the raw and intense relationship between Californians and their landscapes cuts both ways. Only in California would somebody dream up the transforming idea of simply hosing a mountain out of existence in order to gather the gold left behind. Only in California, with its fragile ecology, would it have been possible to find mountains that would evaporate under the pressure of a strong stream of water. Only in California would the result have been such an environmental disaster, leaving behind remnants that still cause problems more than a century later. And only in California would the whole mess be shut down simply because it interfered with another jarring collision with nature.

Given all that, it is perhaps not surprising that California's environmentalists also have an intense relationship with nature. From John Muir on down, these environmentalists have been created in the same hothouse-type environment as the capitalists who developed the state's natural resources, and the result is equally unalloyed.

Just as California's nineteenth-century capitalists had a religious sense of economic destiny, Muir had a religious fervor for nature, a fervor that blossomed in the post–Gold Rush California of the 1870s. Even while making his living as a sheepherder in the Sierras, Muir ridiculed such domesticated livestock as "hooved locusts." And watching the bustling destruction of the California landscape to make way for mines and the towns that supported them, he mused: "Perhaps no such excess of industry was ever before seen in the history of the world."

More than a century later, California environmentalism still carries with it this same kind of raw emotion. To a California environmentalist, it is not enough to manage nature responsibly and harvest a sustainable bounty, Gifford Pinchot–style. To combat the jarring and exploitative collision with a fragile environment like California's, you must defend nature with your very life—lay down in front of a bulldozer, tie yourself to a rock, or at least seek a stay of execution in court with the fervor of a public defender desperately trying to save the life of a death-row murderer.

This brand of environmentalism has, of course, been exported worldwide over the last thirty years. Building on the Muir tradition, California is widely credited with creating and shaping the modern environmental movement, especially after the Santa Barbara oil spill of 1969, which focused the nation's attention on environmental problems. Like the debris flowing down the Feather River toward Marysville, the oil flowing toward the California coastline served as a testament to the notion that colliding with nature cuts both ways, and that the very resources that have allowed California to prosper can swallow it as well.

The resulting approach to environmental protection, with its focus on heavy regulations, bears the unmistakable imprint of the California attitude. If the jarring collision with nature can create legacies like hydraulic mining and offshore oil drilling, the reasoning went, then only an equally uncompromising response can prevent further damage.

Oddly, for a society that has always prided itself on moving so rapidly across open ground, California also has a national reputation for sheer density. The hothouse environment that enabled the state to grow so fast has also incubated laws, regulations, and vested interests unrivaled anywhere else in the West and possibly in the nation. It is hard to move, at least in the political or economic arena, without tripping over something or somebody that can hold you back.

In part, this stems from California's peculiar history as a self-reliant region that has faced the bureaucratic attempts of three different nations to lasso it. Even before the Gold Rush, California was a welter of conflicting claims on land and natural wealth. Then, gold's quick riches instantly created a plethora of vested economic interests, all noisily jostling with one another for advantage. Throughout the twentieth century, California has seen the construction of large-scale public works projects—waterworks, freeways, and so on—that have altered the natural environment for the benefit of these economic interests. And at the same time, the state has seen wave after wave of populist regulation—environmental regulation included—designed to rein the economic interests in.

This historical sequence has quite literally shaped the modern California landscape: the raw exploitation, the massive alteration, and finally the desperate counter-reaction to save what is left. The end result is a society that has gotten better at making sure that bad things don't happen to the natural environment as easily as they used to.

Yet merely preventing the further destruction of California's natural bounty is not enough anymore. After a century and a half of colliding with nature, California is paying a heavy price that is likely to get more burdensome before it gets lighter. All that debris rolling down the Feather and Sacramento Rivers serves as an apt metaphor for the lasting, and still harmful, imprint that California's prosperous society has left on the state's legendary landscapes. Even if we do nothing more to our environment—level no more mountains, divert no more water, extract nothing more from the earth—we will still be left with the fallout of the golden legacy for decades, if not centuries, to come.

That is why it is not enough merely to strong-arm economic forces in hopes of preserving a few remaining pieces of natural California. As we celebrate the sesquicentennial of California, we must remember that we are not living in 1850, when a new arrival from the East Coast could stake out a piece of land along a Sierra stream and start digging. We are not living in 1950, when the roaring industrial economy was chewing up postwar California at an unprecedented rate. We are on the verge of the millennium, and it is time for Californians to act once again on the most basic component of their common identity: their belief in the power of transformation.

For a century and a half, Californians have created and re-created their state in an unbroken chain of events that began with the discovery of gold at Sutter's Mill. They have done it by harnessing their own energy—and the state's potential. They turned hillsides into gold, gold into wealth, and wealth into a society that has been the envy of the world. Now it is time for another transformation.

The next transformation must be one that creates a healthy balance between modern society and the natural environment on which it is built. It must be a transformation that not merely preserves but restores. To succeed, today's Californians must not just believe in this transformation, but also understand the challenge it presents. We must understand the history of our own relationship with nature—how it helped to build the world we inherited, and how it threatens the world we hope to pass on. And perhaps, in the process, we will also learn how to help nature survive those jarring collisions as comfortably as the surfer in a wet suit or the mountain biker with shock absorbers.

The Original California

For most of the world, California began life as a mythical place in a sixteenth-century Spanish romance novel. "Know ye," wrote Garcí Ordoñez de Montalvo in *Las Segas de Esplandián,* "that at the right of the Indies there is an island named California, very close to that part of the Terrestrial Paradise." The island was populated by women who, among other things, kept only a few men for reproduction and then fed the surplus male population to tame griffins. In a particularly fanciful moment, Ordoñez claimed that California "abounds with gold and precious stones."

So it should be no surprise that when Spanish explorers first discovered a real-life paradise not long afterward, they blessed it with a name that already had a golden legacy. It was unlikely that the Spanish would

Ishi, the last Yahi Indian, fishing in the foothills near Mount Lassen, 1914.

California State Parks

stumble across griffins nibbling on young boys at the behest of a group of Amazon-like women. But gold was another story. Gold, after all, was what the Spanish were looking for in the New World.

Eventually, of course, California quite literally became the golden state. But the California that presented itself to the Spanish when they arrived had not been created by a myth. It had been created by a natural history both volatile and elegant, which had left behind a land of rare beauty and dramatic contrasts.

"For an extremely large percentage of the history of the world," wrote John McPhee in *Assembling California,* "there was no California." By this statement, McPhee simply meant that under current geologic theory California was "assembled" by floating pieces of continental plates that drifted toward each other for millions of years before they finally collided. As anybody who has ever experienced a California earthquake knows, they are colliding still—and the state is gradually breaking apart as a result. In the jarring San Francisco earthquake of 1906, the "offset"—the actual movement of earth—was around twenty feet.

Yet McPhee's observation also underscores the fact that California's present landscape was created, in geologic terms, something like the day before yesterday. After the end of the Ice Age—some ten thousand to twenty thousand years ago—the Central Valley consisted of a large sea. So did much of the Mojave Desert, including Death Valley. And San Francisco Bay did not exist as we know it until long after the glaciers receded.

When the Spanish first discovered California, they thought it was an island. In a way they were right. The mountains, the deserts, and the Pacific Ocean create in California a world unto itself. Most of California is dry, and almost all of it is characterized by a seasonal rain pattern—wet in the winter, dry in the summer— found nowhere else in the country. Yet here the statewide similarities end. In most ways California is not one region but a collection of varied locales.

Each of these locales contains, quite literally, its highs and lows. California has within its borders the highest and lowest points in the continental United States. The daily temperature difference within the state— hottest to coldest—often approaches sixty degrees. In just one twenty-mile stretch from San Jose west into the Santa Cruz Mountains, the average annual rainfall rises from thirteen inches to more than sixty.

California's variety, combined with its isolation, has created a unique set of plant and animal species unmatched anywhere else on the continent. Little wonder that the state has its own Endangered Species Act, separate from the federal law. What other state would have to concern itself with the survival of tortoises in a desert, owls in a rain forest, songbirds that thrive in coastal brush, and foxes and hawks that occupy a large, swampy interior plain? And though the modern development of California has left a strong imprint, natural California remains in abundance. Geographers estimate that eighty-six percent of the state's land remains covered with natural vegetation. Not all of these landscapes are original to California—many have been shaped by human hands—but they continue to nurture an array of plant and animal life unequaled in North America.

Despite this still-forming and supposedly fragile environment, California supported more Native Americans, perhaps as many as 300,000, than any other region of the United States. In part, the aboriginal tribes thrived because of the region's Eden-like qualities: a mild climate and what one botanist has called "an extremely variegated, if thinly spread, supply of edible plants and animals." Indeed, California was so much like Eden that many native tribes simply wore no clothes.

In part, however, the native tribes thrived because they adapted successfully to the peculiarities of the California environment. Unlike their counterparts in Arizona, California's native tribes never relied on irrigated agriculture. Instead, they remained semi-nomadic hunter-gatherers until the Spanish arrived in the eighteenth century. Though perhaps as many as fifty tribes lived throughout the state, they mostly concentrated their settlements in areas that could easily support them: the coastal plains along the Santa Barbara Channel and the fertile locales along the Sacramento River and the Sacramento–San Joaquin Delta. And they seem to have achieved a successful balance with nature.

The coastal tribes, such as the Chumash, for example, relied on the fish they could catch from the teeming Santa Barbara Channel. But they were careful not to become over-dependent on this or any other source of food. They also relied on a variety of land-bound plants and animals. And like most California tribes, they gathered acorns as a dietary staple.

Although almost toxic in their natural state, acorns proved endlessly valuable when a little chemistry was applied. So the natives learned to husk, grind, and wash the acorns into a kind of meal, used in almost every dish. The presence of at least ten different types of oak trees brought variety to this otherwise mundane diet.

Acorns were so important to the native tribes that, in this one instance, they were willing to manipulate nature with a somewhat heavy hand. For centuries, the tribes used fire—what we would today call "controlled burns"—to create optimum oak-growing conditions. The burns eliminated underbrush and drove back native chaparral, leaving behind a dramatic landscape of grasslands and large oak trees.

When the Spanish arrived, they found a stunning setting that had been created not just by nature but by the efforts of native tribes to maximize the yield of their hunter-gatherer environment. If California looked like a big park, as many commentators have suggested, that's because it was— an oak-tree park created by the land management practices of the native tribes. The use of fire is just one example of how the tribes thrived, in the words of fisheries expert Arthur F. McEvoy, by "strategically gearing their productive efforts to the ecological realities of the world as they understood them."

Once the Spanish started to colonize California, however, this ecological balance did not survive. Neither did the natives.

Beginning in the 1770s, Spain began an aggressive effort to settle California, motivated in part by their fears that Russia would beat them to it. The Spanish strategy was based on three types of settlements: presidios (forts), pueblos (agricultural towns), and missions. All three played important roles, but it was the twenty-one missions, scattered in coastal areas from San Diego to San Francisco, that came to dominate the Spanish era.

The Franciscan clerics who ran the missions sought to attract the natives to their settlements and convert them to Christianity. But the natives, who had adapted so well to California's natural environment for centuries, did not adapt to mission life. They were forced to surrender their customary nomadic patterns and live in Spanish settlements under almost slave-like conditions. And, like so many North American tribes, they proved susceptible to European diseases. By the time the missions were secularized in the 1830s, most of California's native people had died.

The Spanish era also introduced one of California's most important and enduring traditions: the rancho—which introduced a pattern of almost plantation-style landholdings in which large tracts were concentrated in the ownership of only a few individuals. During the Spanish era, when missions, presidios, and pueblos predominated, only a few large land grants were made to individuals, mostly to Spanish war veterans. Juan Jose Dominguez, a Spanish veteran, was awarded a claim in 1784 after driving cattle onto a tract of land by the mouth of the Los Angeles River. More than two centuries later, much of Rancho San Pedro is still controlled by Dominguez's heirs, who own the Watson Land Company.

After Mexican independence from Spain in 1821, however, the rancho tradition gained a widespread grip on California's economic and social culture. Eager to step up the pace of both settlement and

California State Parks

Dating from 1771, Mission San Gabriel was the first Spanish mission established in what is now the Los Angeles area.

trade, the new Mexican government awarded claims of up to fifty thousand acres to favored landowners. Liberal land-grant laws were adopted, permitting foreigners to obtain property so long as it wasn't located near either the national boundary or the coast.

These policies produced little results in the years immediately after independence. But land grants increased dramatically in the 1830s and especially the 1840s, as Mexico became more desperate to retain control of California. The recipients came not only from Mexico but also from the United States and England, and they began cattle ranching throughout California on a vast scale.

Within twenty years, the business of exporting cowhides and candle tallow made from cow fat had become so successful that the missions were secularized and ranching dominated the state. In many parts of California, Anglos married into local "Spanish" families and settled into a Mexican-style ranching life as "Don Otto" or "Don Bill," pursuing leisure over work. Hence the cowtown reputation of such settlements as Pueblo de Nuestra Señora la Reina de Los Angeles (City of Our Lady, the Queen of the Angels), which as late as 1800 had eight hundred human inhabitants and twelve thousand cows. So important was the trade of cowhides that it formed the basis for California's first literary classic: *Two Years Before the Mast* by Richard Henry Dana, published in 1839.

Despite its highbrow reputation, *Two Years Before the Mast* is mostly a description of commercial vessels shuttling cowhides up and down the California coast—loading thousands at a time on board at Monterey or Santa Barbara or San Pedro for shipment to San Diego, where warehouses held up to forty thousand hides. And in Dana's description, cowhides were so important that they quite literally formed the basis of all economic activity.

"The truth is," Dana wrote after a visit to the provincial capital of Monterey, "they have no credit system, no banks, and no way of investing in money but in cattle. Besides silver, they have no circulating medium but hides, which the sailors call 'California bank-notes.'"

Thus, in isolated Mexican California, there were hints of the California to come. Hides were actually the precursor to gold, a way to convert the state's natural resources into a source of mercantile wealth, a form of currency, and an investment vehicle all at once. And we see an early example of the double-edged sword of economic prosperity in California. While creating a thriving local economy in an otherwise out-of-the-way location, cattle ranching had also "wreaked environmental havoc far out of proportion to the small number of colonists," according to one group of California historians.

Prior to the arrival of the Spanish, California's plains had been covered with native bunch grasses. But the native grasses were quickly—and permanently—crowded out by European species of grass that took root in bare spots between plants. Many of these "invader" species arrived as seeds attached to the straw used by the Spanish for packing purposes. Many more were transported quite literally on the backs of—or inside the digestive tracts of—the livestock brought by the Spanish to graze California's vast open lands. Bunch grasses

The rancho period accelerated the pace of settlement and trade, especially in cowhides and tallow.

that weren't crowded out were devoured by European cattle. And unlike most plant communities, California's native bunch grasses won't return, even if the area is left undisturbed.

"Aside from the deliberate introduction of agricultural and urban development, no other plant community in western North America has changed so much, over such large areas, and in so short a period of time," wrote natural historian Elna Bakker on the effects of cattle ranching on native grasses. In addition, cattle, horses, and sheep eroded the hills, which caused the collapse of stream banks, thus increasing flooding and slides. Many of the deep ravines on ranch land in California today date from this cattle-intensive period.

The environmental effects of ranching increased rapidly in the 1840s, especially as the Mexican government quickened the pace of land grants in hopes of holding off American interest in California, since many of the grantees were Americans and loyal to their country. But the rise in land grants only accelerated the American takeover of the region. Between 1840 and 1846, the non-native population of California grew by twenty percent, most of them Americans. The takeover of California began in 1846, when the U.S. Marines invaded Los Angeles and seized control of the city without firing a shot—largely because they had the support of the local American "Dons." The actual annexation in 1848 was an anticlimax. By then, the Gold Rush had begun, and with it the Americanization of California was triggered in earnest.

Courtesy California State Library, Sacramento

The Golden Gate and the ocean formed California's gateway for trade to the rest of the world during the Spanish and Mexican eras.

The Gold

Among the Anglos who came to control a large chunk of California during the 1840s was a Swiss immigrant named John A. Sutter. An enterprising man hoping to make his fortune, Sutter was typical of the foreigners who came to California late in the Mexican period. Among other things, he facilitated the Russian departure from California by buying Fort Ross, their major North Coast stronghold, in 1841—a feat that brought him favored status with the Mexican government. More important to California history, however, was the fact that Juan Batista Alvarado, the Mexican governor promoting aggressive development, allowed Sutter to set up a virtual empire in the Sacramento Valley.

The Mexicans had not settled the area, but Sutter saw major opportunities for growth, especially along the banks of the Sacramento River and a second river he wishfully named the "American." He persuaded Alvarado to award him an enormous land grant in the area: eleven leagues, or some fifty thousand acres. The governor also granted Sutter civil authority, and with the armaments from Fort Ross, Sutter established de facto military authority as well. Near the confluence of the two rivers he created a small adobe settlement called Sutter's Fort. By 1847 the settlement boasted sixty houses and almost three hundred Anglo settlers, as well as twelve thousand head of cattle, at least ten thousand sheep, and thousands of acres of wheat. Like many of the Anglo settlers at the time, most of the residents were Mormon, and they were supplied by a general store established at Sutter's Fort by an enterprising Mormon elder named Samuel Brannan.

Sutter needed finished lumber to expand his settlement. So he established a sawmill some forty miles up the South Fork of the American River near a place the Indians called Coloma, and he partnered with a valued employee named James Marshall to run it.

The spot was a good one, located near the timber in the Sierra Foothills and along a river that could transport the finished goods to the fort. Building Sutter's Mill required serious manipulation of California's natural environment, however, and this led to some unexpected results. Marshall had to dam the American River and divert the water through a dry channel where the sawmill would be located. By New Year's Day of 1848, the mill and a brush dam were completed, only to be nearly washed away in the kind of winter flood that Sacramentans still struggle with.

That obstacle overcome, Marshall then had to widen and deepen the dry channel to accommodate the timber. At first he used explosives, but he soon found that it was just as easy to simply loosen the dirt in the channel, then leave the sluice gates open at night and allow the river's rushing water to wash the debris out of the channel.

California State Parks

People from all over the world migrated to California after the discovery of gold, making for the only "poor man's gold rush" in history.

On the afternoon of January 24, Marshall saw something unusual. As the great nineteenth-century historian of California, Hubert Howe Bancroft, later related the tale: "While sauntering along the tail-race inspecting the work, Marshall noticed yellow particles mingled with the excavated earth which had been washed by the late rains. He gave it little heed at first; but presently seeing more, and some in scales, the thought occurred to him that possibly it might be gold."

The following morning, according to Bancroft, he went back to check on the previous night's sluicing and noticed "a glitter from beneath the water" and retrieved "a larger piece of the yellow substance than any he had ever seen." He turned it over and weighed it in its hands. He bit it. He hammered it between two stones. And, as Bancroft put it, "the mighty secret of the Sierra stood revealed." Unwittingly, in the process of building a sawmill, Marshall had begun panning for gold, and he had found it.

Despite attempts at secrecy, the news spread quickly throughout the world, at least by mid-nineteenth-century standards. Marshall showed the find to Sutter, who then dispatched a messenger to the governor in Monterey—not to report the news, but rather to reaffirm that Sutter's land title was secure. But the messenger, who had worked alongside Marshall at Sutter's Mill, secreted a few ounces of the precious metal with him and showed it off, first at a general store in Benicia and later in San Francisco. Sutter told a few of his well-connected friends, and his workers began paying for purchases at Brannan's store with nuggets and dust. By March, the first reports of gold were published in San Francisco newspapers, but most readers still dismissed the claim. It was not until sometime in May that Sam Brannan turned up in San Francisco, held up a bottle of gold dust in the street, and shouted: "Gold! Gold! Gold from the American River!"

Brannan's dramatic proclamation set off a rush for the Foothills, first from San Francisco, then from elsewhere in the West, and eventually from almost the entire world. Within a month of Brannan's pronouncement, three-quarters of the population of San Francisco had left town. Sailing crews arriving in the mysteriously depopulated city quickly headed for the hills as well, and soon San Francisco Bay was littered with abandoned ships. By the fall of 1848 it was reported that two-thirds of the able-bodied men in the Oregon Territory had left for California. So compelling were the gold fields that, according to some reports, Colonel Robert Mason, the military governor of California, was abandoned by his staff in Monterey and left to cook his own meals.

By 1849, the word had spread to Mexico, New England, Asia, and Europe, and thousands of young men seeking their fortunes set out for California—some across Panama, some using the rough overland route from Missouri, and some via the eighteen-thousand-mile journey around Cape Horn. This mass migration, combined with the nature of California's gold deposits, made for the only "poor man's gold rush" in history.

The gold was mostly found in placer deposits, easily obtained by sluicing in the rivers or digging along the riverbanks, and it was spread across an enormous geographic area in the Foothills. Neither skill nor money was required to recover the gold. The muddled political situation following the annexation of California to the United States helped to democratize the rush as well. The Mexican government had never doled out land grants in the Foothills, and the Americans hadn't yet created a system for establishing title. The whole region was quite literally wide open.

"There were no squatters, no prior claimants to the gold lands in California," wrote Carey McWilliams a century later, "and since there were no other regulations, it was quite impossible for anyone to acquire title to a mining claim other than by holding it and working it. This made for an enormously *rapid* development, and a truly amazing democracy in production."

Digging, panning, and sluicing, thousands of young men quickly created an industrious landscape unlike anything the world had seen before. So focused were they on the potentially lucrative task at hand that most of them simply overlooked the spectacular natural setting that confronted them. As in many parts of California, north-facing hillsides were lush, while south-facing hillsides were barren. The underlying soil was a surprising red, possibly the result of a lengthy geologic process in which most minerals were "leached out," leaving high concentrations of iron oxide. The lower elevations often supported only grass and scattered oaks; the higher elevations featured impressive pine forests.

Men from around the world worked in their native garb, living in tents or simply sleeping under a blanket. To a certain extent, they lived off the land, harvesting wild onions, feasting on venison, and trying to steer clear of the grizzlies they had heard about. California gold mining was dirty, muddy work that the men tolerated but grumbled about. Whereas the week was spent in search of gold, Sundays were typically devoted to the second most talked-about topic of conversation: laundry. "Have two shirts," one miner wrote. "Wear one until it is dirty. Hang on a limb, exposed to wind, rain, and sun. Put on a second shirt. Wear until dirty. Then change to the clean one."

Within a matter of months, these men had altered the world's economy forever. The California Gold Rush was by far the biggest in history, and it ushered in a whole new era in gold production. Whereas the gold rush of Russia's Ural Mountains had produced as much as 300,000 ounces per year in the 1830s and '40s, California by 1851 was producing ten times that amount, increasing worldwide gold production several-fold.

Back in the gold fields, the miners averaged $20 a day in diggings at first. Because of increased production, the average wage dropped to only $6 a day by 1851; yet this figure was still many times what a young man could make at factory work in the East or farming in the Midwest. Once they had gold in their pockets, the miners were confronted with the problem of what to do with it in such a remote location. And, in a way, here is where the golden legacy really begins.

Since it was virtually impossible to return home with their gold in hand, the miners had to spend it in California. So, like cowhides a decade earlier, gold became the driving force of an entire economy—a tradable commodity with inherent value, a unit of currency, and an investment vehicle all at the same time. "In California," McWilliams wrote, "gold had created a reservoir of local wealth which was used in agriculture, trade, commerce, banking, shopping, and industry." Almost all the great nineteenth-century fortunes of California can be traced back to the Gold Rush.

The first people to really benefit from the Gold Rush were the shopkeepers and suppliers who accepted gold straight from the mines in payment for their goods. After touching off gold fever in San Francisco, Samuel Brannan opened a store at Sutter's Fort and was soon doing $5,000 a day in business. Within a matter of years he became so successful that representatives of Brigham Young arrived in San Francisco to demand a payment of tithe, which Brannan refused, thus "finishing him as a Mormon," at least according to one historian.

Vallejo Street wharf, San Francisco, 1850s. As the closest port to the gold fields, San Francisco exploded with growth.

Courtesy California State Library, Sacramento

Just as successful, however, were those who were shrewd enough or lucky enough to profit from gold as it rippled its way through the California economy. A sophisticated banking system was established almost immediately, as Wells Fargo and other financial institutions grappled with the problem of transporting gold from the mother lode towns back to San Francisco. Gold's wealth was reflected in property values as well. More than a few disappointed miners returning from the gold fields thinking they were penniless were elated to discover that stupendous real estate inflation in San Francisco had made them rich. In more than one case, a property purchased for $15 in 1848 was sold for $40,000 just two years later.

Enterprising middlemen who could secure needed supplies as the goods arrived in San Francisco Bay via ship could make fortunes as well. Collis P. Huntington, who later became one of the Southern Pacific Railroad's monopolistic magnates, gave up placer mining after just a half-day in the fields. But he became a successful Sacramento merchant by cornering the market on shovels, thus laying the foundation for his fortune. At least one account of the period suggested that the most important assets a merchant could have were a good lookout post and a strong pair of oars, the better to spot and pursue cargo ships as they passed through the Golden Gate.

In addition to concentrating a huge amount of financial capital in San Francisco, the Gold Rush also created an enormous market practically overnight for almost everything. This too stimulated the California economy. The early California timber industry got its start from the demands of the Gold Rush. So did Central Valley agriculture. Gold mining later came into conflict with agriculture, as we will see, but the wheat crop was needed to feed the mining camps, the towns, and the growing metropolis of San Francisco. As a result, wheat production grew from seventeen thousand bushels in 1850 to almost six million bushels a decade later.

Even the Southern California cowtowns benefited, because Northern California could afford to pay far more for beefsteak than hide-and-tallow traders could pay for cattle. According to one report, as early as 1852 some twenty-five thousand cattle were driven north from Los Angeles and sold for $30 a head, rather than being sold for hides at $3 each. By 1852 gold was adding close to $1 million a year to the Southern California economy.

With so much capital sloshing around San Francisco, it was inevitable that much of it would be re-invested in the gold-mining industry. And so, within five or six years after the discovery at Sutter's Mill, the "poor man's gold rush" was over. The support systems for gold mining required financial capital. Most gold-mining operations were water-intensive. Diversions were necessary for sluicing and to provide water supplies for the camps. And almost from the beginning, the harvesting of Sierra Nevada timber was necessary to build the diversion flumes and to construct camp buildings.

By the early 1850s, the easy gold had been extracted, and San Francisco capitalists began plowing money into more expensive means of gold production. Mining companies began tunneling to gain access to deposits deep underground. They pursued "quartz mining"—the extraction of gold embedded in quartz, a process that required industrial-strength crushing of the quartz.

Large amounts of Sierra Nevada timber were used to build water diversion flumes to serve the gold fields.

California State Parks

Most significantly, some mining companies began hydraulic mining to extract the rich deposits of gold in the gravel hillsides above the stream banks of the Feather River in Nevada County. The method was invented in 1852 by a miner in Nevada City named Anthony Chabot. Tired of the labor-intensive digging and washing of tertiary gravel with minimal results, Chabot rigged up a hose that would spray a fifty-foot stream of water and tear up the soil, doing the work of twenty men. The debris flowed into a nearby stream and left the gold behind.

Soon hydraulic mining spawned a capital-intensive industry financed by San Francisco investors. Several companies were established just to build reservoirs and canals, and within five years of Chabot's invention, they had built seven hundred miles of ditches throughout Nevada County. This high-tech method kept gold mining alive, giving it a big economic boost in the 1870s and early '80s, when other mining methods had pretty much played out.

Most forms of gold mining had left an environmentally harmful legacy. The streams and hillsides of the Sierra Foothills had been disrupted; even placer mining, conducted by hand, displaced a great deal of mud, sand, and debris. But hydraulic mining operated on a much greater scale. The debris unleashed by hydraulic mining flowed down the Feather and Sacramento Rivers, repeatedly flooding cities and agricultural lands. By one contemporary estimate, hydraulic mining dumped 680 million cubic yards of debris into the streams in a thirty-year period.

For this reason it became the subject of the most pitched political and legal battle in the young state's history, pitting the farmers against the mining companies. Hydraulic mining was finally outlawed in 1884 by Lorenzo Sawyer, a federal judge who had come to California from Illinois during the Gold Rush and mined a stake near Sacramento before beginning a law practice there. It may have been no coincidence that Sawyer was close to railroad magnate Leland Stanford, who saw future profit in transporting grain rather than gold.

By cutting gold production in half, Sawyer's ruling ended a thirty-five-year period that had laid the foundation for California's prosperity and highlighted both the costs and the benefits of the new society. Placer and hydraulic mining left scars in the Sierra Foothills that have proven slow to heal. And while the state was shaped by gold mining, few of the pioneers profited in the end. John Sutter died destitute in a Philadelphia hotel in 1880. James Marshall, who first discovered the gold at Sutter's Mill, lived his whole life near his find, yet he died in 1885 an almost-penniless alcoholic who had spent the preceding decades unsuccessfully demanding compensation for his discovery. Even the merchant Sam Brannan died impoverished in 1889 after a costly divorce, an attempt to finance a revolution in Mexico, and partial paralysis from an enemy's bullet.

By contrast, the "winners" were those who had profited indirectly from the Gold Rush and plowed those profits into new ventures. Though many of these winners were ruthless monopolists who held the state in a fearful grip throughout the robber-baron age, they also laid the foundation for California's future and ushered in a new era when the state renewed its prosperity by harnessing a whole new set of natural resources.

Hydraulic mining removed gold from the gravel hillsides of Nevada County using vast amounts of water, which sent sediment flowing downstream and flooded towns and fields in the Sacramento Valley.

CHAPTER THREE

The Land

I"In the beginning, and always," California's state librarian, Kevin Starr, once wrote, "was the land." Starr went on to call land "the first and last premise of the California experience," and there is no question he was right. Almost from California's discovery, it was the potential contained in the land that attracted the world's attention: the spectacular landscapes, the distinctive grasslands, the vast interior valleys, and eventually, of course, the gold-laden hillsides of the Sierra Foothills. But if it was the land itself that provided the original allure, it was the way that land was owned and traded that created the foundation for modern California.

Throughout the nineteenth-century American frontier, land was used as a way to distribute wealth to people of modest means through homesteading. But in California this tradition didn't hold. After statehood, land in California was secured by private owners in large blocks—usually legally, but often through underhanded means as well.

This pattern of large landholdings, combined with the early creation of capital wealth from the Gold Rush, allowed California to accelerate quickly to large-scale operations in ranching, timber, and agriculture—industries that shaped the modern landscape. About half of the land was retained by the federal government, but much of it was made available for resource use, and so federal lands are also intertwined with the California story.

In part, California's land ownership patterns were created by the sheer scale of the place and by capitalist ambition typical of nineteenth-century America. But the most important element was the simple fact that California's landholding patterns were established by Spain and Mexico, not by the United States, and then carried into the American era.

By the time the United States annexed California in 1848, more than eight hundred large land grants had been dispensed and the Spanish/Mexican rancho tradition had become firmly established, from San Diego up to Sonoma County. When the United States annexed California, it did not void these grants, in large part because annexation's most enthusiastic boosters were Americans and Europeans who had received land grants from Mexico. Under the terms of the Treaty of Guadalupe Hidalgo, which ended the Mexican War, the United States agreed that all property already in private hands should be "inviolably respected."

Native tribes burned the oak forests to increase acorn production, creating grasslands in the process. Early landowners used the oak grasslands for large-scale cattle ranching.

Sweeney/Rubin Ansel Adams Fiat Lux Coll., UCR/California Museum of Photography, University of California, Riverside

But in the midst of Gold Rush fever, many American settlers had no intention of respecting Mexican property ownership. They had endured great hardship in crossing the prairie to get to California, and they viewed themselves, not the landowners, as settlers in the American tradition. They expected to be able to do here what Americans had done for decades in newly opened territory throughout the Midwest and West: stake a claim, establish occupancy, and be rewarded with permanent ownership.

Treaty or no treaty, this is what they did. Thus, most of these settlers were technically squatters, occupying not just land owned by Mexicans, but also land owned by Americans and Europeans, such as John Sutter. The result was a series of confrontations—some violent, some merely rhetorical—intended to pressure the United States to overturn the Mexican property system and legalize the squatters.

In 1850, at the height of the Gold Rush, many newly arrived residents of Sacramento simply began putting up fences, constructing houses, and opening businesses in the riverfront area now known as "Old Sacramento"—land owned by John Sutter and later his successors. Seeking to restore order, city officials evicted some of the squatters and took them to jail, which was located on a ship in the river. The remaining squatters stormed the ship. In the ensuing melee, both the mayor and the city assessor—viewed by the squatters as tools of the landowning class—were killed.

When members of Congress convened in 1851 to consider how Mexican claims should be validated, the demands of these squatters were very much on their minds, as was the question of who should control the richest gold country on earth. Washington had to abide by the treaty with Mexico, of course. But in considering the problem, Hubert Howe Bancroft later wrote, Congress was not thinking of "a quiet, pastoral people, but of a horde of speculators, hungry for gold and power and land; not so much of the valid claims as of the fraudulent ones."

Congress created a lands commission to consider the claims, as well as an appeals process to the District Court and the Supreme Court. To accommodate the squatters' interests, the burden of proof for land ownership was placed on the property owners themselves. Surely, Congress's hope was that this would increase the number of rejected claims, thus opening up more land for small-scale settlement. In fact, it had exactly the opposite effect.

Proof was hard to come by because Mexican record keeping had been casual at best, and many property owners had not abided by the requirements of their grants, such as occupancy. Adjudicating all the claims took almost twenty years—essentially the entire Gold Rush period in California. Far from giving squatters a chance against the big landowners, the lengthy delays and endless legal battles worked to the advantage of those with enough money to buy off the original claimants and keep paying their lawyers' bills.

A speculator named Edward Fitzgerald Beale, for example, gained control of four Mexican land grants during this period and used them as the basis for what eventually became the half-million-acre Tejon Ranch in Kern County. Tejon Ranch is still in existence—now a publicly traded corporation largely controlled, until recently, by the Times Mirror Company of Los Angeles. In the end, about six hundred of the eight hundred claims were approved in favor of the landowners, for a total of almost nine million acres—an average of fifteen thousand acres per claim.

"The real beneficiaries of this twenty-year period of confusion in land titles," Carey McWilliams wrote almost a century later, "were the speculators who, without exception, were American claimants, by assignment, of Mexican grants. The principal victims, of course, were the American settlers or squatters and the original Mexican claimants."

The adjudication of land grants did not lock up all of California for the big landowners, however. There were still some forty-five-million acres owned by the federal government and, therefore, theoretically up for grabs. But because a huge percentage of this land was located in either desert or mountainous regions, it was unsuited for agrarian-style settlement. (Much of this land is still owned by the U.S. Forest Service or the federal Bureau of Land Management.) As it turned out, most of the potentially valuable land fell into the hands of large-scale speculators and capitalists. Why? Clearly, the rancho tradition was so well-rooted in California that both local custom and early state law favored large landholdings. But beyond that, the concentration of financial power created by the Gold Rush, along with the growth and development of the railroad era, made such a pattern inevitable.

It is important to note the vastly different role that the American government played in land ownership and development patterns in the nineteenth century. Today, federal or state ownership usually indicates a desire to keep and preserve environmentally sensitive land, and government agencies often expend large sums of money to acquire the right parcels. But a century and a half ago, when the West was being settled, most people saw the government's role in almost the exactly opposite terms. The federal government owned all the land in emerging territories and defined its job as disposing of that land—to settlers, capitalists, and state governments—in a manner that would maximize growth and development.

As in most other Western regions, the federal government encouraged a "squatting" program, allowing individuals and families to lay claim to tracts of 160 acres and eventually buy the property for $1.25 an acre if they lived on the land and worked it. (An even more generous system was included in the Homestead Act of 1862, which gave land free to squatters who stayed for five years.) The 160-acre restriction was designed to maximize settlement and minimize the possibility of land monopolies.

The 160-acre rule was skirted throughout the West, where it was difficult to subsist on such a small parcel without irrigation. But in California, it seems, the abuses were especially rife. Frontier California was full of stories about drunks, passers-by, and company employees being collared to sign semi-fraudulent land claims for the benefit of large land speculators. Even so, the volume of homestead claims in California was relatively small compared to other parts of the nation, especially the Midwest. And, bowing to California's arid regions, the federal government increased the maximum to 640 acres for desert lands in 1877, creating a program that eventually disposed of about one million acres.

But millions of acres of land also came onto the market without the 160-acre rule. In the late 1850s, the federal government permitted the sale of large swaths of property throughout the West—including eleven million acres in California, largely in the Central Valley—before homesteaders could lay claim to them. This permitted San Francisco real estate speculators to begin accumulating large landholdings. Just as important, however, were the federal government's bequests to the State of California and to the railroads. Both created a vehicle by which speculators could accumulate large quantities of land without technically circumventing federal law.

When California became a state in 1850, the federal government immediately gave the state 500,000 acres for "internal improvements," just as it had with other states. Nineteen days after California's admission to the union, Congress gave the state title to all "swamp and overflow" lands on the condition that revenue from selling the land be used for levees and drains. In 1853, the federal government gave the state two sections in each surveyed township—a total of more than five million acres—to raise money to benefit public schools.

The "swamp and overflow" land program, in particular, was a boon to speculators both shady and honest. In contradiction of federal rules, California state officials interpreted the definition of swamp and overflow land liberally and sometimes allowed private land purchasers to do so themselves. In California such a definition can be stretched much farther than in a territory with less dramatic swings in precipitation. California land that is wet in February may well be dry as a bone—as well as fertile and suited for cultivation—nine months a year.

The temptation to define swamp and overflow land with expansiveness proved great for many land speculators, especially those with their eye on the vast plain of the Central Valley. Legend has it that one of the greatest land barons of the era, German immigrant Henry Miller, hitched a boat to a team of horses and had himself dragged around a dry lake bed to establish his claim to state swampland. Eventually Miller and his partner, Charles Lux, controlled one million acres, including both sides of the San Joaquin River for a twenty-mile stretch. Miller often boasted that he could travel by horse from Mexico to Oregon and sleep on his ranch every night.

Even the federal government's bequests to the state paled in comparison, however, to the land it handed over to the railroads to encourage the growth and development of the state. Hoping to accelerate the race to build a transcontinental railroad, Congress agreed in 1862 to give Western railroads alternate, odd-numbered sections of land on either side of their track.

This led to a checkerboard pattern of land ownership that still exists in many parts of the state today. It was meant to allow railroads to exploit the increased financial value of property alongside their tracks, and to make railroads an aggressive player in promoting economic development in newly accessible territory. In California, it achieved all these goals and more. These land grants were originally given to five different railroads. But within a matter of a few years, all five grants were controlled by one entity: the Southern Pacific Railroad. The Southern Pacific eventually received title to almost twelve million acres of land, more than a quarter of all the private land in the state. Even today, Southern Pacific's successors are among the biggest private landowners in California.

The Southern Pacific combine was created in the late 1860s by a group of moderately successful Sacramento merchants who eventually came to be known as the "Big Four." Collis Huntington, Mark Hopkins,

Courtesy California State Library, Sacramento

Chinese immigrants provided most of the labor for construction of the Central Pacific Railroad through the Sierras.

Leland Stanford, and Charles Crocker started in the railroad business by backing the mercurial Theodore Judah, a young engineer who planned to spearhead construction of the transcontinental railroad. Judah fell out of favor with the group and died an early and untimely death. The Big Four quickly moved in and proved to be ruthless businessmen who dominated late nineteenth-century California like no cabal before or since.

Throughout this period, they worked hand in hand with speculators seeking to assemble large landholdings. Like the state government, Southern Pacific was not bound by the federal government's 160-acre rule. Once the landholding system was in place, the railroad used its money and power to build export markets for a wide range of agricultural products.

The federal government also disposed of almost three million acres of land for timber use and more than 500,000 acres in mineral lands, largely via a system of after-the-fact recognition of claims made by gold miners. In time, the federal government made a practice of husbanding precious land resources for conservation purposes, beginning with creation of Sequoia, Yosemite, and Grant (now Kings Canyon) National Parks in 1890. By the end of Theodore Roosevelt's administration in 1909, federal land ownership had stabilized at about half of the state's acreage. But even this land was often used for other purposes, including oil drilling and mining. Much of the land placed in Inyo National Forest by Theodore Roosevelt was set aside to protect Los Angeles's watershed.

By the time the Gold Rush era ended in the 1870s, the Mexican tradition of large ranches had not diminished. Rather it had grown so much that it began to shape the state's agricultural economy. Because the landowners expected to turn a profit, the California system of land ownership spawned a relentless search for economic gain—

Sheep ranching was one of several large-scale agricultural endeavors that emerged as land-holdings were consolidated in the 1860s.

on the floor of the interior valleys and even in the rocky foothills of the Sierras. This was the genesis of the wheat era, which began about 1870 when the consolidation of large landholdings was complete. The land barons could now take advantage of new railroad lines to export this inexpensive and non-perishable crop. It was also the heyday of large-scale sheep ranching, operated by Basque immigrants who annually herded their sheep from the floor of the Central Valley through the Foothills and into the High Sierras, a practice which would prove environmentally destructive.

While these land-ownership patterns formed the foundation of California's industrial-scale farming and ranching economy, the state paid a price in the form of social instability, especially during the 1870s and 1880s.

Critics of this system were harsh. "California is not a country of farms but a country of plantations and estates," wrote Henry George in 1871. "Men have grown rich, and men still make a regular business of blackmailing settlers upon public land, of appropriating their homes, and this by power of the law and in the name of justice." George himself had resorted to begging on the streets of San Francisco to support his family, and his California experience was the basis of his seminal treatise, *Progress and Poverty*, which questioned the morality of financial gain from speculative landholdings.

Even sympathetic observers believed that the state had too quickly settled into a Southern-style plantation pattern with a permanent laboring underclass of Chinese, Mexicans, and poor whites. And all too often, this pattern was reinforced in violent confrontations between small-scale settlers and large-scale speculators.

Perhaps the most famous incident was the violent confrontation in Mussel Slough in 1880, between landowners who had purchased property from Southern Pacific and squatting farmers who believed the railroad had never legitimately owned the land. The farmers had created a successful small-scale farming community by growing hay and by cultivating specialty crops using water from the nearby Kings River for irrigation. When the Southern Pacific brought its line to the area, however, the railroad claimed large blocks of land and sold the property off to speculators. When the speculators arrived to claim their property, the unarmed farmers resisted and a half-dozen were killed.

The incident later formed the basis for Frank Norris's famous anti-railroad tirade, *The Octopus*. Describing a railroad map of California in the novel, Norris calls the red-marked routes of Southern Pacific as "an excrescence, a gigantic parasite fattening upon the life-blood of an entire commonwealth."

Southern Pacific's monopolistic power over the state was eventually overturned by the Progressive movement in the early twentieth century, and it has often been criticized since. But had it not been for Southern Pacific's efforts, there would have been little cultivation of any kind in the Central Valley. Even "politically correct" histories of California have recently recognized the railroad's legacy in a more evenhanded way. Social conditions have never been ideal in California's farming regions, but the state's landownership patterns have also served as the foundation for its agricultural productivity. And it may also provide the basis for modern conservation opportunities as well.

The Magic Liquid

Land has always been California's most basic raw material, but water has been the elixir that brought the state to life. Originally California was a vast seasonal waterscape, overflowing in winter and spring, then drying up in summer and fall. During the Spanish and Mexican eras, the modest requirements for water use were met with small-scale irrigation. But in developing the state's resources after 1848, water truly was "the magic liquid." And over the past century and a half, the state's growth has been shaped not just by water or just by land, but by the combination of both. In the words of Joseph Jensen, an influential Los Angeles developer from the 1920s through the '60s, "Land is just land until you put water on it."

During the state's early development, the control of water and the control of land went hand in hand. In the twentieth century, California had to take a more communal approach to water development. But by then, the pattern of water rights created in the nineteenth century—like the pattern of land ownership—had already laid the foundation for modern California society.

Mark Twain is often quoted as saying that in the West, "whiskey is for drinking and water is for fighting over." The truth is a little more complicated. Although water was scarce in places, simple scarcity was not the biggest obstacle to California's development. Rather, it was the uneven distribution of water—over time and over geographic space—that inhibited large-scale growth.

Large portions of the Central Valley and Southern California were semi-arid lands; some were true deserts, receiving only a few inches of rain per year. But other conditions more than made up for this lack of precipitation. The North Coast forests measured their rainfall in feet. The winter snowpack in the Sierra Nevadas often contained an enormous amount of water that became available every spring when the snow melted and flowed down into the Central Valley. And even the

Small-scale agricultural irrigation at Mission Santa Barbara

arid lands stored huge quantities of water underground, some of it built up over centuries.

In building California, the problem was not the amount of water available, but finding ways to use the water where and when it was needed to suit the needs of a growing society. Water conflicts were rare during California's Spanish and Mexican era because community irrigation had been common practice in the arid parts of Spain and Mexico. It was only with the Gold Rush that intense competition for water began—stimulated partly by the needs of the mining industry and partly by the introduction of European ideas about water rights, which emphasized the rights of individual landowners.

From the start, gold mining in California was a water-intensive activity. Because placer gold appeared in streams and in riverbanks, early gold mining consisted of little more than manipulating the flow of water to reveal it. It was by diverting water through a dry channel that James Marshall first noticed gold at Sutter's Mill. Later, large flumes were built to bring even more water to the gold fields.

But given the crowding of the gold fields, how should this scarce resource be allocated? Miners, who were accustomed to respecting the rights of those who had staked the first claim, quickly adapted this concept to the allocation of water and developed the notion that came to be known as "first in time, first in right." This concept, also known as "prior appropriation," stated that the first miner to use the water had the right to continue using it, and if he stopped using it, he then lost the right to it.

Prior appropriation was given legal validity in 1851, when the state legislature ratified existing mining customs. But it was not the only philosophy with legal backing. Even before it swept mining customs into state law, the California legislature, like most other states, adopted the principles of English common law. Among these principles was the concept of riparianism, the idea that the owner of a riverbank was entitled to the full natural flow of a river or stream. Upstream owners could remove water for domestic use but not for irrigation.

California Department of Water Resources

Hetch Hetchy Reservoir in Yosemite National Park

Developed with the lush countrysides of England in mind, riparianism was ill-suited for a semi-arid region with seasonal stream flows and a growing dependence on irrigated agriculture. But it was well-suited for the emerging pattern of large-scale land ownership. Even during the wheat era of the 1860s and 1870s, the land barons understood that whoever controlled the water would profit the most. Many landowners, such as Henry Miller and Charles Lux, shrewdly concentrated their holdings along riverbanks, especially in the Central Valley. Then they asserted riparian water rights as a means of wresting the river's water away from whomever had been using it under the doctrine of prior appropriation.

It was not long before irrigation-oriented farmers both large and small complained that the riparian philosophy was "repugnant." In a landmark legal battle in the 1880s, a Kern County irrigator named James Ben Ali Haggin took on Henry Miller and Charles Lux, hoping to overturn the riparian approach. In 1886 the California Supreme Court eventually reached a compromise that stated that landowners (including public landowners) did have riparian rights, but that the doctrine of prior appropriation applied if an upstream owner had withdrawn water from the stream before the downstream owner had asserted his riparian claim. "Put simply," wrote Norris Hundley Jr., California's preeminent water historian, "both systems were legitimate and timing determined which prevailed in a conflict."

A diversion flume bringing water to a gold-mining operation

Courtesy of Pacific Gas and Electric Co.

Courtesy of Kern County Museum

Early diversion of water for farming near Bakersfield, 1889

Los Angeles Dept. of Water and Power

"There it is. Take it." The first water from the Owens Valley arrives in Los Angeles's San Fernando Valley, 1913.

The *Lux v. Haggin* ruling was not popular because small farmers wanted a clean victory, one that eliminated riparianism altogether. But it did force the next stage in California water history: a reliance on communal irrigation. The 1880s and '90s saw a rise in farm populism nationwide, and because wheat crops had depleted the California soil, farmers were increasingly switching to irrigated agriculture and new cropping patterns. Populists in the California legislature hoped that establishing irrigation districts throughout the Central Valley would create public accountability for water use and force the breakup of large landholdings.

In some areas, including Los Angeles County, small-scale vegetable farming did emerge, and within just a few years California was leading the nation in irrigated agriculture. But on the whole, the large landowners continued to prevail, while numerous local irrigation districts failed. Many Central Valley land barons started using ground-water to water their fields. By the 1920s, this trend made California the leader in farm production, but it did not secure the state's long-term agricultural future. "Farming advanced in California during the early decades of the twentieth century," Hundley wrote, "but there was always a tenuous quality about it, especially for those in the Central Valley and including even the large landowners." Stability would have to await large-scale water development.

By the early twentieth century, the federal Bureau of Reclamation was promoting such stability throughout the West with dam-building and irrigation projects. In California, however, the great cities mastered water development long before the farmers did, establishing both partnerships and rivalries that persist to this day.

The most famous example was Los Angeles's successful effort to tap water sources in the Owens Valley and divert it southward more than two hundred miles to quench the thirst of the growing city. The sordid nature of this tale has been exaggerated by fictionalized accounts such as the movie *Chinatown,* which depicts it as a conspiracy among greedy landowners hoping to open up the San Fernando Valley for agriculture and development. This particular conspiracy has never been solidly proven, but there was a good deal of underhandedness.

Los Angeles secured the rights to tap the Owens River during the first few years of the twentieth century, not the least because of the duplicitous efforts of a former mayor posing as a rancher and a Reclamation Bureau official who was secretly in his employ. The resulting Los Angeles Aqueduct, built under the direction of self-taught water engineer William Mulholland, was a two-hundred-mile marvel, using only gravity to transport the water through the Mojave Desert. When the first water flowed through the sluice gates in San Fernando in 1913, Mulholland dramatically declared: "There it is. Take it." Los Angeles's growth brokers did just that, using the water as necessary raw material to create one of the world's greatest cities. Later, all the cities of Southern California banded together to build another aqueduct, this time to the Colorado River, two hundred miles to the east. This aqueduct would fuel the region's great post-war suburban boom.

San Francisco's tale of liquid imperialism is not as well known, but it's no less dramatic. As early as 1902, just as Los Angeles was laying its plans for the Owens River, San Francisco devised a plan to dam the Tuolomne River at the beautiful Hetch Hetchy Valley, 170 miles to the east. At the time, San Francisco was unquestionably the most important city in the West, but the plan met strong opposition from a peculiar alliance of private water companies fearful of losing business and the strident environmentalist John Muir. The Hetch Hetchy Dam required federal approval because it was located in Yosemite National Park. Congress finally passed the bill in 1913, but water did not start flowing through the Hetch Hetchy Aqueduct until

San Francisco Public Transportation Commission Photography Department

John Muir opposed the construction of O'Shaughnessy Dam, claiming the Hetch Hetchy Valley was as beautiful as Yosemite Valley.

The Oroville Dam under construction in 1964. Located on the Feather River in the Sierra Foothills, the dam provides water storage for the State Water Project, which transfers water to farmers in the Central Valley and cities in Southern California.

1934, more than twenty years after the Los Angeles Aqueduct opened. The Hetch Hetchy project assured San Francisco's dominance over the Bay Area; the city still makes millions every year by selling water and power to its neighbors. But the length of the battle played a major role in Los Angeles's successful effort to overtake San Francisco as the leading city in the West.

During this period, the great landowners of the Central Valley also sought to build vast water development projects. In the 1920s, as concern over the depletion of groundwater increased, support slowly grew for a project whose centerpiece would be a dam on the Sacramento River near Redding, 160 miles north of Sacramento. The project won narrow voter approval in 1933, in the midst of a severe drought. Coming during the Great Depression, the project proved too costly even for the state government, and it was taken over by the federal Bureau of Reclamation. The Central Valley Project, or CVP, eventually came to include five major dams from Redding to Fresno with canals carrying water in all directions.

But there was a major price that the Central Valley's landowners had to pay in order to obtain federal assistance for the CVP: the Reclamation Bureau rule that restricted recipients of federal water to owning only 160 acres of land—the same restriction that had been contained in the Homestead Act. The nineteenth-century land barons had circumvented this restriction by illegal dummy land purchases. In contrast, their twentieth-century successors fought tooth and nail in Congress all during the New Deal for the repeal of this restriction. Eventually, the Reclamation Bureau settled the matter by permitting "technical compliance" with the law, achieved by distributing land ownership and/or water rights among corporate stockholders, relatives, or farm employees.

The final piece of California's water mosaic came in the 1960s, when the state initiated its own project. Called the State Water Project, it included the damming of the Feather River near Oroville and the construction of the California Aqueduct, providing water for landowners in the southern San Joaquin Valley and for municipal use in the Los Angeles and San Diego areas. The $1.75-billion bond issue for the State Water Project, which was championed by Governor Pat Brown, was barely passed by the voters in 1960. The project was never completed, however, portending a new era of scaled-down ambition and increased competition for water in California and throughout the West.

As originally designed, the State Water Project included a "peripheral canal" to carry water around the Sacramento–San Joaquin Delta, a move that even some environmentalists said might improve the health of the Delta by ending the state's practice of pumping water through it to the California Aqueduct. In 1982, however, the voters rejected the Peripheral Canal plan, and it has never been seriously revived.

The Peripheral Canal defeat was a defining moment of how water is used in California. Since then, Los Angeles has been forced to reduce the amount of water it siphons from the Owens Valley in order to restore the fragile environment of Mono Lake. And California is cutting back on its use of Colorado River water because of increasing water demands from Arizona and Nevada. Even San Francisco has felt pressure to tear down Hetch Hetchy Dam, which some environmentalists say is not needed to serve the city's water and power needs. Today, both farmers and urban areas are feeling more pressure than ever to re-think their use of the "magic liquid"—thus allowing more of it to flow toward the sea in ways that will replenish the state's natural water systems.

CHAPTER FIVE

The Trees

As soon as Californians began extracting gold from their rivers and riverbeds, they went to the mountains and started felling the giant trees as well. The lumber was needed to support the mining operations, providing raw material for sluice boxes and the vast flume systems that were soon developed, and also for building mining camps and the towns that sprang up nearby.

Before long, the wealth created by the Gold Rush allowed the timber industry to take on a life of its own. The demand for high-quality building products in prosperous San Francisco fueled a need for lumber. Later, a bustling foreign market was developed, and then large quantities of timber were required to build California's railroads. The peculiar difficulties in harvesting and transporting the timber led to a heavy reliance on San Francisco capital and the city's port facilities, and, in the longer term, to a heavy concentration of absentee land ownership, which set the stage for future conflict.

Typical of California's dramatic topographical contrasts, the state's vast forests were concentrated in specific geographic areas. At the time of the Gold Rush, the Sierra Nevadas held large stands of pine and fir, as well as magnificent giant sequoia redwoods. Along the coastline, an even larger belt of coast redwoods stretched some four hundred miles from Sonoma County almost to the Oregon border, with secondary forests farther south in the Santa Cruz Mountains. Both these "tall forests" sheltered within their canopied darkness a remarkable array of wildlife, ranging from crested jays to Roosevelt elk (on the North Coast) to the infamous spotted owl.

The Gold Rush consumed large quantities of lumber from the Sierras. Later, Sierra logging grew rapidly to meet the demands of railroad construction throughout the state and, indeed, throughout the Great Basin, which was virtually barren of trees. Simply building snow-sheds for the railroad eastward through the Sierras required 300 million board feet. The Comstock silver-mining operation, just over the state line in Nevada, took 70 million board feet per year from the Sierras. By the mid-1880s, it was estimated that a third of the Sierra forests had already been cut—mostly pine, but increasingly the giant sequoias as well. It was this fact, as much as anything else, that led the push to create Yosemite and Sequoia National Parks in 1890.

Logging on the North Coast was mostly for export to San Francisco, the East Coast, and foreign markets. And whereas Sierra timber was the backbone of industrial development, the coast redwood was promoted as the ideal material for high-end housing markets. One promotional

The redwoods were so large that even experienced lumberjacks were not capable of felling one alone.

Jeff Gnass

Spring grasses and oak woodland, Middle Fork Kaweah River Canyon, Sequoia National Park

book from the 1880s recounts the tale of a farmer who noticed that the redwood boards he had bought for fencing were so beautiful that he used them for the interior finish of his house instead.

Coast redwood trees were such awe-inspiring examples of natural creation that even the capitalists who harvested them sometimes had second thoughts about doing so. Many towered hundreds of feet in the air, with a diameter of twenty feet or more. The largest redwood ever felled produced enough lumber to build twenty-two five-bedroom houses.

"These majestic John the Baptist cedars seem to possess a magic power over passing fogs," rhapsodized one forest expert a century ago, in typical Victorian prose, "precipitating them, and as it were, sprinkling with a continual rain on the loose ashy earth."

The sheer size of the coast and sequoia redwoods, along with the vast stands of other trees in the Sierras, meant the amount of available timber was enormous. In the 1880s, even after a third of the Sierra forests had been cut, the state government estimated California's total supply of timber at around twenty-five billion board feet. This was a conservative estimate; most logging experts figured the actual number was four or five times that amount.

In both the Sierras and the North Coast, the rough terrain and peculiar topography required a whole new way of logging. In other parts of the country, trees were clear-cut, then shipped to sawmills by floating them downstream along adjacent rivers. In the East and the Midwest, the

Because rivers were small, California logging required significant capital investment in transporting logs via railroad and other means.

rivers were large and the gradient from the mountains to the flatlands was gentle. And once the forests were cut, the land would then be farmed by homesteaders.

California, however, was different. The trees were bigger, the rivers were smaller, the rainfall was seasonal, and the slopes were much steeper. Simply felling a giant redwood was a task that tested the skills of the most experienced lumberjacks, while getting the trees out of the forest seemed practically impossible.

Floating them downriver was a risky affair; the riverbeds were steep and treacherous and, during the dry season, there was not enough water to carry the logs. Sometimes it took two to three years for the logs to make it downstream. Sawmills were often built at an elevation of three thousand to four thousand feet, thus creating the additional problem of how to transport the cut wood down the hill to market.

Solving California's peculiar timber problems was capital-intensive and, ironically, usually involved the consumption of huge quantities of timber. To get the felled trees out of the forest via oxen, the loggers invented the "skid road"—a corduroy-like road made up of smaller cross-logs along which a log would roll, or "skid." Even in the nineteenth century, a skid road could cost as much as $5,000 a mile to build. And it could only be built in the spring, after the rain had stopped, even though the timber might have been harvested many months before.

The North Coast was scattered with small communities that were built up around sawmills.

In the Sierras, many logging operations and sawmills stood high above where railroads could run, and so the logs had to be sent down the hill along complicated wooden flume systems, which used an enormous amount of wood to build and cost up to $135,000 a mile.

On the North Coast, getting the logs out of the forest was even more complicated. They couldn't be floated downstream to a central point, because there was no single large river system. Instead, they had to be transported down a series of short, steep, fast-running rivers straight to the sea. Once there, the logs had to be loaded at a port, which was small and expensive to operate. There were few natural harbors on the North Coast—only what the loggers called "dogholes." As one forest historian wrote, "The loading of ships alongside the jutting headlands was accomplished only by sending the timber thundering down long apron chutes that jutted out over the cliff edge and into the hold of the vessel waiting below."

The capital-intensive and isolated nature of California logging meant that San Francisco emerged as the most powerful logging center on the West Coast. In addition to being a major market for timber, it was the only place in the West with enough money to finance the logging operations. And, except for Seattle, it was the only harbor big enough to serve as a transshipment point. Virtually all logging ships leaving Humboldt Bay on the North Coast went to San Francisco, and all the North Coast logging companies had lumber yards and trading offices there. Even Seattle was largely built as a logging center by San Francisco capitalists.

The early pioneers of California logging, many of them from the Midwest, were wood-cutters who focused on building and operating sawmills. But the capital-intensive nature of the business soon forced the creation of a concentrated ownership structure that included timberlands as well as mills. Capitalists investing such large sums of money needed to be assured of a long-term return, and the only way to guarantee it was to control the source of timber as well as the manufacture of wood products.

Obtaining the land, however, was not easy. There were no large private landholdings on the North Coast. Only two Mexican land grants had been deeded here, and both were rejected by American authorities. In the 1860s and '70s, investment groups on the North Coast, much like their farming counterparts in the Central Valley, went to great lengths, most of them illegal, to circumvent the federal government's 160-acre

California State Parks

The North Coast had no natural harbors—only small "dogholes" where lumber companies built apron chutes to send the logs thundering onto the ships.

California State Parks

Before the invention of tractors, mechanical "steam donkeys" were used to speed the process of moving felled lumber out of the forest.

limit to qualify for inexpensive land purchases. "Farmers were stopped on their way home," noted one observer, "and merchants were called from their counters and persuaded to allow their names to be used to obtain land." The federal government sold land for $1.25 an acre; the value of redwood timber was often a thousand times that amount.

By the 1880s, however, the capital requirements proved too great even for San Francisco investors, and the sawmills and timberlands of the North Coast were marketed to wealthy Eastern and Midwestern timber men. By 1905, twenty-five companies controlled three-quarters of California's timberlands. Half of these companies were located in the East or Midwest, and even those that were officially headquartered in California were controlled from elsewhere. The Pacific Lumber Company, based in the "company town" of Scotia, had a reputation for decades as a benevolent family-owned business—but the family was originally from Detroit. The only truly Californian company among the big landowners was Southern Pacific, which controlled about one million acres of forest.

The deep pockets and concentrated ownership of the California timber industry proved both good and bad for the forests. From the beginning, California logging practices included considerable wastage. For example, it took three thousand board feet of redwood tree to obtain one thousand board feet of redwood product. Early loggers sometimes left three-foot-tall stumps, which increased the likelihood of fire. And shake makers basically strip-mined the trees, cutting only the pieces they wanted.

To overcome the California-specific challenges to logging, the big timber companies aggressively pursued technological advances, often to the detriment of the environment. Beginning in the 1880s, they started using steam "donkeys," devices capable of lifting and moving big trees around the forest. The donkeys made the clearing of felled trees faster and more efficient, and soon the timber companies had to replace oxen with railroad lines.

By about 1909 the typical California logging operation had become highly mechanized. "The railroad extended to the mouth of a gulch where a landing 200 to 300 feet long was situated," wrote logging historian Howard Melendy. "Here was the bull donkey, and skid roads branched out up the various gullies. At the top of each road, small donkeys yarded the logs into loads of 15 to 30 and then dragged them to the landing by the heavy donkeys, which loaded them on the train."

And this was only the beginning of environmentally destructive mechanization. After World War I, the timber companies began to make heavy use of the Caterpillar tractor, which had been invented by Stockton entrepreneur Benjamin Holt. The "Cat" rendered the donkeys obsolete because it could simply "ground-skid" trees directly from the stump after they were cut.

On the other hand, the concentrated land ownership patterns of the timber industry actually facilitated early conservation efforts. The timber companies had so much capital tied up in their land that they abandoned the idea of farming or ranching it after it was clear-cut. Therefore they went along with the state's initial efforts at forest management in the 1930s and '40s, which held the promise of future second-growth yields. Unfortunately, this was not sufficient preparation for the pitched battles of the 1980s and '90s over whether to harvest the remaining old-growth forests on the North Coast.

CHAPTER SIX

The Farms

The Gold Rush played a key role in jump-starting California's lumber industry, but it was even more important in forming the basis for the state's approach to agriculture. Not only did the Gold Rush create the market demand and capital wealth required for an emerging agricultural industry, but it also was a key source of both labor and ingenuity for the huge farms that would dominate the valley below the gold-laden foothills.

Within two decades of the Gold Rush, agriculture had become a major force in the state's economy. And it had done so in characteristic California fashion: It was capital-intensive, highly mechanized, concentrated in its land ownership patterns, and oriented toward export markets. This basic structure never changed, but it did evolve over time, readily absorbing new ideas from around the world about labor, about markets, and especially about unusual, high-value crops.

Carey McWilliams, who was a California agriculture official as well as a writer, once drew up a list of worldwide influences on the state's crops. It included plums from Japan, alfalfa and walnuts from Chile, flax from India, avocados and tomatoes from Mexico, dates from Algeria, Egypt, and Persia, figs from Turkey, pears from China, prunes from France, and a lima bean developed by the Hopi Indians. By the 1920s, food crops had become California's new gold, and the state passed Iowa as the leading agricultural region in the country.

California's dramatic and varied topography meant that large portions of the state, especially the rugged mountains, were unsuitable for farming. But the valleys, both along the coast and in the state's interior, held great potential for agriculture. The coastal areas had the warm days and cool nights that were perfect for produce. Some of the smaller interior valleys, like Napa, proved excellent for growing wine grapes, while the desert-like climate of Southern California was ideal for citrus fruit.

The wheat harvest on this ranch in Yolo County required a thresher pulled by 33 horses.

Department of Special Collections, University of California Library, Davis

The centerpiece of California's agricultural potential, however, was the Central Valley—a dry and mostly hot plain stretching some four hundred miles from north to south and encompassing the drainage systems of both the Sacramento and the San Joaquin Rivers. It was on this vast canvas that California agriculture was created, dramatically altering some of the state's most distinctive natural features in the process.

The northern half of the Central Valley—the Sacramento Valley—was familiar to most Californians because it provided the transportation routes, the staging areas, and the support towns for the gold fields during the Gold Rush. So it was not surprising that the Sacramento Valley, which had large plains and an ample supply of water from the Sierras, emerged as California's first significant farming region.

Most gold diggers did not get rich quick and soon tired of the backbreaking, muddy work. Many, especially those from the Midwest, had rural backgrounds and soon settled down on their own farms. Many more provided the itinerant work force required by the agricultural industry.

At first agricultural progress was slow, but in the 1860s better information about weather patterns was developed, and the Central Pacific Railroad began aggressively promoting agricultural exports. It was during this period that California's first great agricultural empires emerged: the vast wheat farms of the Sacramento Valley. Wheat was the perfect crop for the Valley, because it was suited to dry weather, it wasn't perishable, and it lent itself to the profitable economies of scale that the export-oriented California capitalists sought.

By providing ready access to export markets, the railroads stimulated a centralized, industrial-style structure among the wheat growers; indeed, oftentimes the wheat growers simply started farming wherever there were railroad lines. The biggest wheat empire was pieced together by Hugh Glenn, a dentist financed by San Francisco capitalists, who built a 55,000-acre wheat farm in Colusa County. Like other wheat barons, Glenn harvested his fields with gigantic "gang plows" that required up to thirty-five horses to operate. His harvest was so voluminous that Southern Pacific ran "wheat specials" just to pick up his grain. And Glenn's empire was so vast that after his death his landholdings formed the core of a new county named in his honor.

By the latter part of the nineteenth century, California was the leading wheat producer in the world, hitting a peak of forty-one million bushels in 1890. Wheat made the agricultural sector so strong—and so closely tied to the powerful railroads—that agriculture eclipsed gold mining as the state's most powerful political force. When hydraulic gold mining was banned in 1884 because sediments washed down the rivers interfered with farming practices, it was the combined clout of Sacramento Valley wheat farmers and railroad interests that brought about the prohibition.

The wheat era did not last long. Relentless cultivation quickly depleted the soil, and competition soon arose from the Mississippi Valley and also from Russia. The wheat industry was more or less wiped out by the economic panic of 1893. But by then, the vast wheat empires had laid the foundation for the economic structure of agriculture in California. They had also stimulated technological advances, such as steam combines and tractors. Two other trends, large-scale irrigation and the push toward specialty crops, would work to bring agriculture once again to the forefront of California's economy.

Irrigation had always been key to farming in California. But because of the doctrine of prior appropriation, there was no guarantee that downstream users would have access to water, even if they owned the riverbanks. This led many farmers, especially in the San Joaquin Valley, to use groundwater for irrigation.

By the 1920s groundwater overdrafting was so severe that, at the growers' request, both the state and federal governments initiated large-scale water projects to provide a steady and more equitably distributed source of irrigation water.

While the organizational structure of agriculture came from the top, many of the innovative ideas for what crops to cultivate came from the bottom—from the hired farm workers who have always tended California's fields. In a century and a half, California's farm laborers have been drawn from a remarkably diverse population, ranging from Chinese to Japanese, Filipinos, Mexicans, Okies, and African-Americans. The history of race and ethnic relations in the fields has not been a happy one, and more often than not one group or another has been driven from the industry by xenophobia. Yet the contributions of each group have become a permanent part of California agriculture.

The Chinese provide a particularly good example. Chinese immigrants played an important role in early California, in the gold mines, on the railroad lines, and in the wheat fields. According to the 1860 census, one in ten Californians had been born in China, and by the mid 1880s—the height of the wheat era—Chinese made up half of the state's farm labor. But other immigrant groups, such as the Irish, resented the Chinese workers willingness to work for low wages. In 1885, anti-Chinese riots erupted throughout the Sacramento Valley, from Redding down to Dixon, and thereafter the Chinese retreated to urban areas or small rural enclaves, such as the town of Locke in the Sacramento Delta. They were replaced in the fields mostly by the Japanese, and the cycle started all over again.

Over the years, many other ethnic groups have worked in various aspects of California farming—not just unskilled laborers, but knowledgeable farmers as well, from regions as diverse as Armenia, Portugal, and the Basque region of Spain. The California wine industry, for example, was started by a Hungarian nobleman seeking a dry climate as relief from asthmatic attacks. Agoston Haraszthy came to California in 1849 and planted what is known today as the Buena Vista Vineyards in Sonoma County. Were it not for these various ethnic groups, it is unlikely that California today would have such diverse and seemingly recession-proof crops, ranging from wine grapes to rice to sugar beets to almonds.

Many crops were nurtured for export by the Southern Pacific Railroad, which bankrolled small start-up farms, gathered weather and precipitation data, and conducted groundbreaking research on refrigeration. New crops were furthered promoted by another distinctive aspect of California agriculture: the growers' exchange. These exchanges, such as Sunkist, encouraged farmers to pool their resources and work together in developing export markets and preservation techniques.

As with timber, the capital-intensive, industrial-style approach to agriculture both demanded—and facilitated—what one commentator has called "a sharply alienating, intensely managerial relationship with nature." This is true most everywhere agriculture has flourished, but it is especially true in the Valley.

"People generally look on it as the garden of the world or the most desolate place in Creation," wheat baron John Bidwell once said of the Central Valley. There is no question that, to nineteenth-century eyes, the valley floor was a barren place: flat, hot, hazy, often devoid of familiar vegetation, and full of unexpected misery. Crossing through Pacheco Pass from San Jose into the Valley in the 1860s, the early surveyor William Brewer expected a crystal-clear vision of the Sierra Nevadas in the distance. Instead he got a dust storm. "Dust

As this photograph of a grape harvest shows, California's farm laborers have always been drawn from a remarkably diverse population.

Keystone-Mast Collection, UCR/California Museum of Photography, University of California, Riverside

The growth of California agriculture was stimulated by the invention of refrigerator railcars and export-oriented marketing techniques.

fills the air—often we cannot see fifty yards in any direction—it covers everything," he wrote in his journal. "We cook our dinner but before it can be eaten we cannot tell its color because of the dirt that settles on it."

Amid this misery, however, the Valley was a richly varied tapestry of nature on a grand scale, with abundant wildlife and vast waterscapes that ebbed and flowed in harmony with nature's rhythms. As recently as a few thousand years ago, the Central Valley was an inland sea. Early native creation tales recall "a world of water." When the Gold Rush–era surveyors and land barons came upon it, it was still, in many ways, a volatile, water-based ecosystem.

The Central Valley could be wet or dry, depending on the annual rainfall and the size of the melting Sierra snowpack. Traveling from Sacramento to Stockton in 1861, a year of normal precipitation, William Brewer's party encountered bothersome mosquitoes and tarantulas. Attempting the same journey the following year, after a winter with some fifty inches of rain, Brewer was unable to cross the swollen San Joaquin River.

Particularly distinctive were the water and drainage systems of the southern San Joaquin Valley, the site of present-day Tulare, Kings, and Kern Counties—today among the top twenty agricultural counties in the nation. These counties are not part of the San Joaquin River drainage system, but rather are part of a natural "sink" originally known as the Tulare Basin. The Kings River flowed into Tulare Lake, which typically covered some twelve square miles in southern Kings County. During the rainy year of 1862 the lake swelled to more than sixty times its normal size, making it the largest freshwater lake west of the Mississippi. According to one account, the area around the lake "was then a land of contrasts: vast reed beds, swamps, and lakes surrounded by bleached grassland or land with no grass at all."

Southern California proved well-suited for large-scale citrus production. Growers' exchanges such as Sunkist allowed growers to pool their resources.

The Kern River, meanwhile, terminated at Buena Vista Lake near present-day Taft. In its natural state this area was more like a seasonal delta than a river. "The area that would become Bakersfield," writer Gerald Haslam once noted, "was known as Kern Island—a complex of distributory channels, sloughs, and marshes."

Such a rich and volatile environment, though commonly written off as "miserable" by the local settlers, created a spectacular setting for wildlife. The literature of the Central Valley, especially of the Tulare Basin, is filled with references to wildlife in almost unbelievable numbers. Even the most casual observers were astounded by the vast skeins of geese that darkened the sky or by the huge grizzlies that roamed the Valley. Camping along the Kern River in 1848, between the present-day locations of Fresno and Visalia, J. W. Audubon reported:

"Today I ran on to a herd of about 1000 elk; so close was I that I could see their eyes perfectly; these elk must be greatly harassed by wolves [coyotes], which are very numerous, and so bold that we have had several pieces of meat, and a fine goose stolen from my tent door. Their long, lonely howl at night, the cries of myriad of wild geese… and the discordant note of the night herons, tell the melancholy truth all too plainly, of the long, long distance from home and friends."

The reclaimed land in Kern County was used for irrigated farmland and oil exploration.

Obviously, an environment teeming with wildlife and susceptible to extreme water fluctuations could not be cultivated in its natural state. Over time, the water flows in the Central Valley were tamed to suit the steady rhythm of agriculture rather than the ebb and flow of nature or the needs of wildlife. "Wild open lands were quickly subdivided, settled, fenced, and plowed in rectangular patterns," wrote the authors of the classic California history, *The Elusive Eden*. "Wagon tracks and country roads marched out along the second lines, accentuating the geometric order being imposed on the land. In keeping with 'efficient' land management practices, natural watercourses were drained, filled, plowed over, or diverted to irrigation. Farmers with large plows and graders leveled the undulating land into the flat planes suitable for straight furrows, irrigation, and large farm machines."

After Benjamin Holt's invention of the Caterpillar tractor, California farming left horses behind.

Before long, islands in the Sacramento Delta were diked to prevent flooding. But the islands' spongy peat proved resistant to heavy farm machinery, so Benjamin Holt of nearby Stockton invented the Caterpillar tractor, which laid down its own track and picked it up as it went, allowing farming throughout the Delta. By the time massive state and federal irrigation projects were started in the 1930s, the entire Central Valley had become a managed environment organized to suit the needs of farming.

As California continues to grow wealthy from agriculture, only an echo of the Central Valley's natural ecosystems remain. In a few places, like the Sacramento Delta and the Yolo By-Pass near Sacramento, fields still flood in wet years—admittedly the result of modern management practices—attracting an abundance of wildlife. Some species of birds, foxes, and other animals still range across vast swaths of the Valley, coexisting with cultivated crops. Rough estimates suggest that perhaps only two to five percent of the region's original wetlands remain. In places like "Kern Island," the alteration of the natural environment has been so extreme that it has been eradicated from local memory. "No other section of this great trench has been more dramatically altered by humans than this one, which, in terms of popular perception, has actually ceased to exist," Haslam has written.

These alterations have had a ripple effect on the broader natural environment as well. The diversion of water for both farming and for cities in the Central Valley has starved the Sacramento Delta and threatens the San Francisco Bay. Because it is still a natural sink with no outlet, the Tulare Basin's conversion to agriculture caused a whole slew of secondary problems—selenium contamination, for example. But after a century and a half of shaping the Central Valley to suit the needs of agriculture, Californians today at least understand that some reshaping is necessary, not just to restore the natural environment but also to protect the future of this fertile plain.

The Kern Island Canal and other man-made water diversions tamed the volatile watercourses of the Tulare Basin for farming.

CHAPTER SEVEN

The Ocean

From the time Europeans first began to colonize it, there was a sense that California was somehow different from the rest of the New World—more full of potential and more able to take advantage of the opportunities that presented themselves. And what gave it this rich sense of possibility—what made it *California,* rather than Montana or Colorado or Arizona—was the ocean.

California's land was filled with beauty and bounty, but it was the presence of a varied and dramatic 1,100-mile coastline that gave California a special magic. To begin with, the coastline itself is a spectacular natural setting. Almost half consists of rocky shore with cliffs and bluffs, while the other half wends its way around bays, lagoons, and tidal creeks.

Just as important, however, was the fact that the Pacific Ocean gave outsiders easy access to California at a time when sea travel was the only way to cover long distances quickly. It may have been eighteen thousand miles from Boston around Cape Horn to the Golden Gate, but even at that distance, it took less time to travel by ship than to travel overland, making California much closer to Eastern capital and supplies than the Western interior. And so the ocean was the key to unlocking California's treasures early and establishing the region quickly as a strong trading partner with the rest of the world.

More than that, the coast and the ocean gave California much of its natural diversity as well. In contrast to the East, the rugged coastline provided so few natural harbors that even in the hide and trading days ships had to drop anchor a mile or two offshore. Yet California had always been blessed with spectacular coastal environments that supported a remarkable and diverse range of aquatic life.

The California coast has long been known for its variety of marine mammals—whales, dolphins, sea otters, sea lions—which can be seen near the shore and around the islands in the Santa Barbara Channel. The rocky portions of the coast hold not only breathtaking vistas but also thousands of tidepools teeming with life. California's greatest natural estuary—San Francisco Bay—boasts rare

California's undeveloped coastline was incredibly scenic—even in San Pedro, now site of the Port of Los Angeles.

Sandstone headlands south of Davenport,
Santa Cruz County

tidal mud flats built up over centuries. Along the North Coast, as in the Pacific Northwest, many species of salmon use both the coast and the freshwater streams, creating one of the great salmon fisheries of the world. And coastal wetlands up and down the state have traditionally provided a subtle and unique set of natural resources.

Not surprisingly, Californians have used these coastal resources extensively over the past century and a half, and the ocean has played an irreplaceable role in the state's economic development. Yet those who have not been careful have paid a heavy price. Even more than land-based resources, California's coastal resources are finite. Without good stewardship, they are easily depleted, as generation after generation of Californians have learned.

Of all of California's native tribes, only the Chumash, who occupied present-day Ventura and Santa Barbara Counties, used the sea extensively. Skilled at constructing many different kinds of canoes, they shuttled nomadically between the mainland and the Channel Islands. Among these canoes was the massive *tomol,* made of driftwood, which could weigh up to two tons and carry a dozen people. In keeping with their general orientation toward living within their ecological means, the Chumash fished extensively, using hooks and nets, and collected shellfish for both food and ornamentation. They even used some marine mammals for food, including seals, sea otters, and dolphins.

Conversely, California's first non-native settlers used the ocean's resources not for survival but for economic gain. A massive hunt for sea otters began in the eighteenth century when Russian explorers discovered that the seals' dense fur—650,000 hairs per square inch—fetched a high price in Chinese markets. The Russian fur-hunters established a military outpost at Fort Ross, in present-day Sonoma County, and although they mostly hunted along the North Coast, they often raided southern waters—sometimes as far south as Los Angeles—without permission from the Mexican government. Modern estimates suggest that the Russians took between 50,000 and 150,000 sea otter pelts during the thirty years they controlled Fort Ross, and perhaps as many as one million pelts before sea otters became almost extinct at the end of the nineteenth century.

The first whaling ships left from Monterey in 1854. The whalers hunted both the humpback and the California gray as the whales traveled on their annual migrations to and from Baja California. These giant sea mammals were hunted principally for their oil, which was used in lamps. By the 1870s, whale oil production reached as much as four thousand barrels a year. But the industry's growth was limited by the whale population itself, which in turn was limited by the hunters, who hunted mostly females and their young. By the turn of the century, as California's whale population declined, public support for hunting them also declined. Tarry oil, made from cow fat rendered into tallow, had emerged as a new energy source, and sailing ships now transported shipments of tallow along the California Coast.

By this time, the ocean's role as California's freeway of the nineteenth century was firmly established. Where natural estuaries existed, they were used as gateways to inland California—fostering the state's economic growth, but also harming the fragile ecologies of the estuaries. Where estuaries did not exist, towns and cities grew up along the coast anyway, building wharves as their connections to the sea and the rest of the world.

Of all the California's estuaries, none was more important, both economically and ecologically, than San Francisco Bay. Yet its role in the growth of California did not come quickly. Remarkably, European

The rapid growth in shipping during the gold rush kicked off a century of dredging and filling San Francisco Bay.

explorers had overlooked the Golden Gate Bay for more than two hundred years, beginning with the first exploration by the Spanish in 1542. It was not until 1769 that an overland party of Europeans noticed the connection to the sea. After the advent of the Gold Rush, the Bay became one of California's greatest assets—a navigable window to the world whose great expanse permitted the creation of several major ports, including San Francisco and Oakland.

By contrast, Los Angeles had an important natural estuary in Santa Monica Bay but chose not to use it as a port. Since the hide and tallow days, San Pedro, located some thirty miles south of Los Angeles, had been the city's connection to the sea. When Los Angeles entered its modern era of urbanization in the 1870s, local power brokers who favored the port at San Pedro won out. After a pitched battle with Santa Monica, they obtained federal subsidies for the dredging of a deep-water harbor. A century later, the area south of Los Angeles would have twin ports—San Pedro and Long Beach—which together form the most powerful shipping and trading center in the United States.

In both Los Angeles and San Francisco, the development of the ports meant a disruption of the natural ecology. San Francisco Bay was a complex estuary, actually part of a larger ecosystem that included the Sacramento–San Joaquin Delta, the rivers in the Central Valley, and the streams of the Sierra Foothills. Saltwater and freshwater engaged in a constant push and pull within the San Francisco Bay system. As a result, an enormous amount of sediment has been deposited over the centuries along the edges of the Bay, creating tidal areas that contain both mud flats and salt marshes. These areas may seem untidy, but they are ecologically significant. Along with the rest of California's coastal wetlands, they support hundreds of thousands of waterfowl, ducks, wading and diving birds, sustained by the vast populations of crabs, clams, and worms that live under the mud.

From the Gold Rush on, this ecological interconnectedness has played a vital role in the health of the San Francisco Bay. When debris from hydraulic mining increased the sediment and the water level in the Sacramento River, it also harmed the Bay by creating sandbars along its upper reaches. Later, the construction of the Central Valley Project and the State Water Project significantly cut the flow of freshwater into the Bay, altering its ecological balance and encouraging saltwater intrusion deeper into the Bay-Delta system.

Most dramatically, rapid development of the entire Bay Area triggered massive fill projects by San Francisco, Oakland, Berkeley, Richmond, and all the other cities surrounding the Bay. Today, two airports, numerous wharves, and endless urban developments sit on fill so old that, in many cases, municipal officials literally do not know what material it is made of. In the century after the Gold Rush, the fill efforts were so great that the estuary we know today is significantly different than the one early settlers saw. The current bay is two-thirds the size and half the depth of the original bay, and it contains only about five percent of the tidal wetlands. The Bay might have simply become a memory—replaced by a kind of San Francisco River—had the state not created the Bay Conservation and Development Commission in 1965 to regulate dredging and filling.

The Chinese initially developed the Monterey Bay fishery, only to be removed later to make way for Cannery Row.

If the history of the San Francisco Bay is the story of a natural resource whose depletion was halted just in time, the story of sardine fishing in Monterey Bay is not. Though Monterey Bay has been rejuvenated by both public and private efforts in recent decades, it still carries the wounds of an industry that consumed resources so aggressively that they were soon gone forever.

The natural riches of the Monterey Bay were well known to explorers and settlers of the Spanish and Mexican eras; Monterey was, after all, the provincial capital up until the Gold Rush. But in those days the commercial value of its fisheries was dwarfed by the far more profitable hide and tallow trade, which dominated both California shipping and the Monterey economy at the time.

Ironically, it was not until the Chinese were forced to seek other areas of work in the 1870s that the commercial opportunities of the Monterey Bay fisheries became evident. Chinese laborers had emigrated to California in large numbers during the Gold Rush, but they were driven from the gold mines and then from the agricultural fields by racism. And after 1869, with the completion of the transcontinental railroad, they were no longer needed as railroad laborers. So the Chinese retreated—some to urban "Chinatowns," as in San Francisco, and others to promising but overlooked oceanfront locales where they could re-create the fishing villages of their native China.

One such locale was a rocky point just south of Monterey called Point Alones (Abalone Point), which was renamed "China Point," after the Chinese built a shantytown and began to develop a successful fishing economy. "A small fleet of colorful, one-oared sampans and jump-like sailboats roamed the waters of the Bay hauling in squid, abalone, and various other sea creatures," wrote Monterey Bay historian Tom Mangelsdorf. "After the squid had been caught, they were strung on poles or laid out on racks to dry in the sun. Open fields surrounding the Chinese village, adorned with heavy laden drying racks, took on the appearance of a patchwork quilt."

The Chinese salted the squid and exported it to China. They also exported fresh fish to San Francisco and by 1900 their thriving fishing economy was worth some $200,000 a year, proving the viability of commercial fishing in Monterey Bay. Perhaps it is no surprise that the reaction to the Chinese was no different than it had been in the gold fields. In 1906, their landlord, the Pacific Improvement Company, tried to evict

Fishing trawlers off the California coast

them. A massive fire, which may have been arson or simply a fortuitous event for the landlord, destroyed the entire village. In any event, the Chinese were soon gone.

In their place rose a distinctive set of buildings that would eventually become the most important, and most famous, sardine-canning district in the world. *Sardinops caerulea* was found in abundance in Monterey Bay, and several entrepreneurs were experimenting with canning techniques. During World War I, when canned sardines from the Mediterranean were no longer available because of the fighting in Europe, Monterey's "Cannery Row" boomed. The city's aspirations as a resort community were dwarfed by the economic power of the canneries.

At the height of production during World War II, Cannery Row had some two dozen canneries squeezed into a four-block area. "Cannery Row," wrote John Steinbeck in his best-selling novel of the same name, "is a poem, a stink, a grating noise, a quality of light, a tone, a habit, a nostalgia, a dream." When Steinbeck's book was published in 1945, Monterey's Cannery Row was also a remarkable economic machine. Fishermen delivered 237,000 tons of sardines to the canneries that year, producing 1.6 million cases of sardines, 34,000 tons of sardine meal, and 8.3 million gallons of sardine oil. Sardines represented approximately eighty percent of California's total commercial catch.

Then, mysteriously, the sardines vanished. By 1948, the total tonnage had dropped by more than ninety percent, to only seventeen thousand tons, and the industry never recovered. The California Fish and Game Commission had warned against overfishing for more than a decade, but the commission's attempts to restrict the catch had repeatedly failed. It is unclear whether the precipitous drop was due to overfishing or whether there may have been other factors that contributed, such as toxic pollution. In any event, it is a cautionary tale of the exploitation of natural resources. "Cannery Row committed economic suicide," wrote historian Mangelsdorf. "The sardine industry grew too quickly, improved its technology too superbly, and pulverized and squeezed too many sardines into meal and oil instead of canning them reasonably for human consumption. The sardine supply yielded its abundance for too many years until the human capacity to harvest the fish far outstripped the sardine's ability to reproduce."

Cannery Row may be one of the most startling examples of the finite nature of California's ocean's resources, but it was more recent development along the coast—oil drilling and housing construction—that has led to some of California's most stirring environmental activism.

Offshore oil drilling and human habitation have maintained an uneasy coexistence along certain parts of the California Coast, especially the Central Coast, for more than a century. From Ventura up to Pismo Beach, oceanfront communities have lived for decades alongside oil wells, storage tanks, and pipelines. After World War II, however, the offshore oil industry began to expand dramatically, particularly in the Santa Barbara Channel. The channel, a fifteen-mile-wide stretch of deep water between the Santa Barbara–Ventura coast and

A commercial fishing dock

William Neill

the Channel Islands, is a major fishery, an important route for migrating whales and dolphins, and a rich location for aquatic wildlife.

Offshore drilling in state waters has been restricted for decades, but in the 1950s and '60s more than a dozen offshore rigs were authorized and built in federal waters. Though most of these rigs have been operated safely, a major oil spill in 1969 had an electrifying effect on the American environmental movement. Blowouts on the Unocal rig began in January and the spill was still not under control by Christmas. Tens of thousands of barrels of oil washed ashore, and at least 3,600 oil-tarred birds perished in the tragedy.

The Unocal spill is credited with mobilizing a new generation of environmentalists in the United States and prompting the passage of both the National Environmental Policy Act and the California Environmental Quality Act. Furthermore, the spill occurred at about the same time that Californians became alarmed over the acceleration of resort and second-home development in coastal areas up and down the state. So it was, perhaps, not surprising that the state's voters approved Proposition 20—the Coastal Act—in 1972.

The Coastal Act sought to manage both onshore development and offshore resource use by creating the California coastal Commission, which has served as one of California's most aggressive environmental agencies for the last quarter-century. Though the commission has always been controversial, its existence attests to the continuing desire of Californians to accept the undeniable limits required to maintain and restore the coastal and ocean resources.

California Department of Conservation, Division of Oil, Gas and Geothermal Resources

Texaco Platform Helen off the Santa Barbara coast

Morning clouds and pampas grass, Big Sur Coast

CHAPTER EIGHT

Under the Ground

*I*n 1866, only eighteen years after James Marshall's discovery at Sutter's Mill, there was little question in anybody's mind that the most valuable substance under California's earth was gold. But this fact did not dissuade a twenty-five-year-old wildcatter named Thomas Bard from drilling into a hillside near Ojai to look for something else.

After several tries, Bard finally struck oil—a well he called Ojai No. 6, which was soon producing fifteen to twenty barrels of oil a day, making it the first profitable oil well ever drilled in California. Bard's discovery came only seven years after the drilling of the first successful oil well in Pennsylvania, and it came at a time when there were only a few practical uses for oil in California's then-embryonic industrial economy.

Ojai No. 6 proved to be a powerful agent of change for Bard, for Ojai, and ultimately for California. Within five years, Bard had become the most powerful politician in Santa Barbara County. Within ten years, the economic clout created by Ojai No. 6 and its successors had forced Santa Barbara to carve an entirely new

Many of California's earliest oil discoveries came as the result of hand-digging by prospectors.

Security Pacific Collection/Los Angeles Public Library

county—Ventura County—out of the hillsides and coastlines where the emerging oil fields were located. In 1890, Bard and several colleagues gathered in a small office in nearby Santa Paula to form the Union Oil Company of California. A decade later, he was elected to the U.S. Senate, playing a key role in the Progressive-era attack on the Southern Pacific Railroad.

Within a half-century of Bard's success in Ojai, oil had created in California a different kind of society, a society driven not by coal or wood but by oil and natural gas. Despite its isolated location, California was self-sufficient in its fuel consumption, and it was perfectly positioned to exploit the economic opportunities presented by the introduction of the automobile.

The story of oil is just one example of how the history of California has been shaped by a vast array of mineral resources. As the modern consumer society emerged, Californians of all backgrounds fanned out across the state in search of the raw materials required to sustain it. A second wave came in the twentieth century when California needed to industrialize to meet growing military needs. Many minerals other than gold—oil and borax chief among them—played an important role in creating California's prosperity and its strong sense of self-identity. This legacy has shaped many of the conservation challenges facing the state today.

As gold played out, the next major extractive industry in California was fuel—specifically oil and gas. By 1916, oil and gas accounted for almost half of all mineral production in the state; by the 1960s, the figure had risen to about two-thirds. It was the production of oil and gas that permitted California to emerge as a twentieth-century powerhouse. And it was the environmental side effects of oil production, in particular, that stimulated the modern environmental movement in California.

Fuel had always been a problem for settlers in early California, in large part because there were only limited supplies of coal and wood in many parts of the state. In the nineteenth century, this lack of conventional fuel resources drove California toward the widespread and innovative use of wind power. They accounted for up to forty percent of California energy use in the late 1800s. Windmills were especially crucial for pumping groundwater. Some Salinas Valley farmers used wind power to push sixty feet underground for water, and the farming center of Stockton was known as the "city of windmills."

In the forty years after Bard's discovery at Ojai, enterprising Californians found vast stores of oil, especially in the Tulare Basin, the Los Angeles area, and the coast and hillsides around Santa Barbara and Ventura. In 1892, an unsuccessful gold and silver miner named Edward Doheny noticed that Los Angeles residents used tar for fuel, their source being what later became known as the La Brea Tar Pits. Knowing nothing about the oil business, Doheny dug 150 feet down by hand, fashioned a crude drill from a sixty-foot eucalyptus tree to push even deeper, and struck oil after forty days. A few years later, oil entrepreneurs began dotting the sandy beach at Summerland, just south of Santa Barbara, with oil wells. And in 1899, two men named Elwood, who ran a small lumberyard in Bakersfield, struck oil in a hand-dug hole at seventy-five feet.

Within a decade, California had become the leading oil-producing region in the world, producing about twenty-five million barrels of oil a day. Two-thirds of it came from the extremely rich Kern River oil fields that the Elwoods had stumbled upon with their hand-dug hole. Oil fields became a common sight everywhere in California. "Even as the train whizzes by," wrote the editor of the *San Jose Mercury* when he traveled through Summerland in 1901, "one sees streams of black, syrupy-looking oil pouring out from the pump's mouth with the heavy flow and reluctant slowness of molasses running from a barrel on a cold morning."

This high level of oil production provided crucial economic independence as California approached a period of massive growth. At the time, the United States depended on coal for about seventy percent of its fuel needs. Californians, on the other hand, relied on oil for eighty percent of their fuel, virtually all of it locally produced. Because California had enough ingenuous wealth to finance much of the oil production, and because by 1900 there was already an in-state market of more than a million people, California never established a colonial energy relationship with the East Coast, as did so many other western states. In this sense, the story of oil in California, as with so many natural resources, is really just a continuation of the events set in motion by the Gold Rush.

In classic California fashion, the local oil proved to be a resource that was difficult to extract and process, thus requiring large capital investments and technological innovations. California oil was, for the most part, a sticky, tar-like substance. In its raw form, the "asphaltum" near the surface had been used by native peoples for a variety of purposes. Its unusual viscosity, however, caused a series of problems.

CA Department of Conservation, Div. of Oil, Gas, and Geothermal Resources

A pumping rig near the Huntington Seacliff Country Club in Huntington Beach.

*Oil seepage at Rancho La Brea, located near
present-day Wilshire Boulevard in Los Angeles*

In the nineteenth century, the main commercial use of oil was as raw material for making the kerosene used in lamps. But refining the sticky oil was difficult. California oil became more viable only after Evan Edwards, a Ventura storekeeper, developed a new type of oil burner that used a jet of steam to atomize the oil and direct the fine spray into a furnace.

Transporting the oil was also a problem, which, characteristically, led to innovative solutions. Carrying oil on ordinary ships, the traditional method, proved too difficult because of leaks, so Californians developed the first oil tanker. A few years later in 1902, Standard Oil of California (now Chevron) started building the first long-distance oil pipeline, stretching 275 miles from the Kern River oil fields to its refinery in Richmond, near San Francisco. But moving the molasses-like liquid through the pipeline wasn't easy. Standard Oil quickly concluded that heating the oil to 180 degrees Fahrenheit helped move it along. But when the oil cooled after about ten to fifteen miles, it stopped moving. The first shipment of oil went into the pipeline in Bakersfield in March and did not arrive at the refinery in Richmond until July.

*Islands in Long Beach Harbor
constructed to support the oil industry*

Then there was the problem of water. Oil and water don't mix, of course, but the peculiar geology of the California fields made it difficult to keep them apart. Petroleum experts understood that water seepage could ruin a good well by transforming a profitable flow of crude oil into a worthless flow of contaminated water. Elsewhere in the country, water was usually found at a shallow depth, with hard rock separating it from the oil below. Drillers could use the natural rock as a "ledge" to separate the oil from the water. In California, however, there was no such easy separation of oil and water.

The area of the Kern River oil fields was characterized by sandy soil, the result of thousands of years of seasonal flooding. Water and oil lay essentially together amid the sand, and separating them was not easy. Early drillers typically abandoned wells that were ruined by water seepage. This practice just made matters worse, facilitating the flow of water from one property to the next. In the Kern oil fields, water seepage became such a problem that production dropped by twenty percent in 1905, severely threatening the oil industry at the very height of California's first oil boom. This led to the state's first oil-drilling regulations, which required abandoned wells to be boxed in containers to prevent water from seeping elsewhere.

The mining of "Twenty Mule Team Borax" from Death Valley didn't have as strong an influence on the state's growth as oil did. But it is still an important chapter in the California saga. Like oil and countless other resources, it required large amounts of both capital and ingenuity to unlock.

In the late nineteenth century, the usefulness of a salty substance known as borate of soda was just beginning to emerge as an important building block of the industrial society. By preventing rust, borax could be used in nickel plating, pottery making, hide tanning, meatpacking, and the construction of that newfangled miracle, interior plumbing. Soon it would become a staple component of soap and laundry detergent as well. Because borax had such a huge soap market, the Harmony Borax Company decided, in the 1870s, that it would be worthwhile to mine the borax found on the floor of Death Valley.

Transporting the manufacturing materials into Death Valley was difficult enough, as shippers charged the company eight cents per pound for the three-week, 250-mile overland journey from San Bernardino.

Many early Southern California oil fields were located in areas that had already been subdivided for houses and small farms.

Oil seepage along the coast near Carpinteria, where oil wells were poorly capped early in this century.

Finding fuel to keep the operation going was even harder. Workers scoured the desert with shovels, digging up mesquite wood that had been buried in sandstorms. But getting the finished product out of Death Valley—across two enormous mountain ranges and 165 miles of unrelenting desert to the nearest railhead in Mojave—was the toughest task of all.

    This trek took both mules and men twenty days to cover, almost three weeks with no shade, water supplies spaced ten miles apart, and vertical climbs and descents approaching four hundred feet per mile. Simply building a road ten miles across Death Valley required the backbreaking task of hacking and molding the salt flats into a makeshift path. (Like most drudgery in early California, this task was accomplished by Chinese laborers.) To create profitable economies of scale, Harmony demanded that special wagons be built that could carry ten tons of borax at a time. This led to the innovative concept of pre-weathering and pre-shrinking wood. Otherwise the wagons would dry out, shrink, and the wheels would loosen in transit. The wagons alone weighed three tons each, and the typical mule team hauled three wagons at a time.

According to California historian W. Storrs Lee, "Commanding a twenty-mule borax wagon was something like sailing a full-rigged schooner single-handed, using an oar for a rudder." Not surprisingly, the rate of damage was high—for the mules, the men, and the borax, if not for the wagons, which turned out to be remarkably sturdy. Accidents occurred when the mule teams hurtled out of control down a steep grade—pushed, essentially, by the weight of thirty tons of borax. According to Storrs, another wagon might come along in few days, "to shovel away the drifts of spilled borax from the tangle of wreckage, put a few mangled animals out of the last of their misery, and bury the dead." Then again, another wagon might not come along for months, for washouts, rocks, and debris constantly altered the route to Mojave.

In the best California fashion, it wasn't long before a clever entrepreneur, Francis M. "Borax" Smith, cornered the borax market and turned the whole saga into a marketing device. He put a picture of the twenty mule team on the label, boasted about the 165-mile journey through 130-degree heat so that his product could provide "economy and labor saving for the housewife."

The mining of borate, talc, and other minerals continues in various parts of the California desert to this day. Most geologically promising parts of the state show the signs of mineral extraction, whether old mining flumes in the mountains, defunct oil wells on the beaches, or deserts pockmarked with the dreams of prospectors and speculators.

While these efforts have created great wealth for California, they also left behind a mixed environmental legacy. Even as wells and mines shut down, the problems have not gone away. Latter-day mining activities used toxic chemicals that still pose problems for the state's natural ecosystems. And a century after the first drilling on the beach at Summerland, oil seepage remains a problem. More than four hundred improperly capped wells are scattered along the beach and in the ocean—many shut down with a blast of dynamite and then plugged with an old telephone pole. With mineral resources, as with other natural resources, California is beginning to recognize the conservation challenge that a century and a half of development has left behind.

"Twenty Mule Team Borax" traveled 165 miles from Death Valley to the railhead at Mojave—a trek that took almost three weeks.

Seepage from beachside oil wells at Summerland, near Santa Barbara, remains a problem almost a century after the wells were capped.

The Foothills

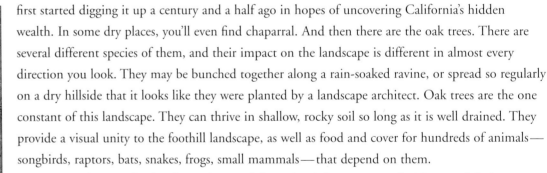

When you head out of the Sacramento Valley east toward the High Sierras, it's easy to overlook the fact that the terrain around you is changing as you begin to climb. You tend to focus on the flatness of the valley behind you—and, by contrast, the overpowering majesty of the Sierra peaks ahead of you. But as you head upward—moving, for example, from the suburbs of Sacramento past the Folsom Lake reservoir and into El Dorado County—before you know it you are in a different kind of place.

It's a hilly, rolling landscape—unusually gentle for dramatic California, yet full of surprises. You'll see rocky outcroppings here and there, and in many places cattle still graze on the annual grasses, which long ago drove out the native perennials. The soil is red—oxidized—just as it was when the '49ers first started digging it up a century and a half ago in hopes of uncovering California's hidden wealth. In some dry places, you'll even find chaparral. And then there are the oak trees. There are several different species of them, and their impact on the landscape is different in almost every direction you look. They may be bunched together along a rain-soaked ravine, or spread so regularly on a dry hillside that it looks like they were planted by a landscape architect. Oak trees are the one constant of this landscape. They can thrive in shallow, rocky soil so long as it is well drained. They provide a visual unity to the foothill landscape, as well as food and cover for hundreds of animals—songbirds, raptors, bats, snakes, frogs, small mammals—that depend on them.

This may be the closest thing California has left to a savannah. It's an undulating, tree-dotted territory located just a few miles from where James Marshall first discovered gold in the American River in 1848. The landscape is duplicated up and down California's Gold Country, from Auburn down to Jackson and beyond. Without the farming potential of the flat land or the dramatic allure of the mountains, the Sierra Nevada Foothills were mostly a memory after the gold fields shut down more than a century ago. No rush of population moved in to claim them; no flurry of government action was set in motion to preserve them. The Foothills, by and large, belonged to longtime ranching families and individuals who sought a rural refuge from California's urban bustle.

Now, the Foothills have been discovered again—not just by conservationists who understand the value of the oak-pine forests and the ecosystems they encompass, but also by commuters and retirees who want to live amid the Foothills' scenic splendor and rural atmosphere. Yet the very atmosphere these new residents seek is being threatened by the influx of people. The gold

Blue oak in the southern Sierra Foothills

Fred Hirschmann

William Neill

Oak trees, Mount Diablo State Park

George Ward

Lupine and oak trees in spring, Ishi Wilderness, Lassen National Forest

California poppies and valley oaks,
BLM Hollister Resource Area, Fresno County

diggers may have been trespassers on federal land in the nineteenth century, but today virtually all the property in the foothill counties belongs to private landowners. No substantial conservation preserves exist. Many of the oak-pine woodlands in the Foothills were subdivided decades ago, and lot owners expect to be able to build homes. Many other areas are now being carved into large-lot subdivisions—five, ten, twenty acres—that are too small to support grazing or conservation activities. For all these reasons, the Foothills, after decades of being overlooked, have emerged as one of California's greatest conservation challenges.

Though the oak-pine woodlands are the dominant ecosystem of the Foothills, they are actually intermixed with other natural communities—chaparral, for example. Oak-pine woodlands are found in many places surrounding the Central Valley, but here in the Foothills the oaks have recently become the major focus of conservation activity. This is partly because of the trees' scenic allure and because of the pivotal role acorns played as a staple food for native tribes in aboriginal California. But mostly it is because the oak is a classic indicator species, whose own health can be used to measure the health of the entire ecosystem that surrounds it.

One reason that oak-pine woodlands are so diverse—appropriately enough for a savannah-like setting—is that the circle of life found here is unusually complex. Ecologists say that there are three types of symbiotic relationships found in nature. Some organisms are mutually dependent upon each other; others live off their partners without hurting them; and still others—parasites—live at the expense of their partners. The oak-pine woodland is one of the few ecosystems that encompasses all three of these symbiotic relationships. "Things live on things which live on things," as one California naturalist has put it. The blue oak–foothill pine woodlands of El Dorado County support more than forty sensitive plant species, ranging from the Mount Diablo manzanita shrub to a dozen or more herbs.

The plants and animals that depend on this ecosystem don't rely just on the oak trees—as woodpeckers do when they eat acorns—but on the oak-pine woodland environment as a whole. Saving just the oak trees themselves won't necessarily preserve the many other natural systems that are dependent on them. Because the various natural communities within the oak-pine woodlands are interdependent upon each other, it is necessary to preserve these important connections. Ecologists at the California Department of Forestry and Fire Protection estimate that removing only five percent of the foothill oaks could eliminate as much as forty percent of the valuable oak-pine woodland habitat, doing great damage to the plant and animal species that live there. Ecologists call this the "halo" effect, because the removal of one oak spreads the damage to the habitat all around it.

Over the past twenty years, the rate of population growth in California's foothill counties has outstripped all the coastal areas and the Central Valley as well. More than 600,000 people now live in the Foothills. Many towns have doubled in population, or nearly so, since 1980. The population of the Foothills counties today exceeds the bulge of humanity they were forced to accommodate at the height of the Gold Rush in 1852.

The dynamics driving this rapid growth vary from place to place. Upper counties such as Placer and El Dorado—site of the original gold rush—are filling up with Sacramento commuters. The lower counties such as Calaveras and Tuolomne—the so-called "mother lode" counties—are attracting retirees and

Fred Hirschmann

Gold Rush town of Angels Camp, preparing for its annual frog jumping festival

Jeff Gnass

Autumn morning along the South Fork of the American River, where gold was first discovered in 1848

Spring wildflowers brighten a boulder-strewn meadow,
Butte County

Jeff Gnass

dropouts from the Bay Area and Southern California. Alone among California's rapidly growing regions, the Foothills are attracting immigrants from elsewhere in the state, rather than from other states or from foreign countries.

All this growth has strained the natural environment. In the last half-century, more than one million acres of oak-pine woodlands have been lost in California, and that figure is estimated to be increasing by nearly fourteen thousand acres per year. Unfortunately, the impact on the ecosystem as a whole is probably far greater, since the subdivision patterns in the Foothills promote the halo effect. As state ecologists have pointed out, the pattern of development is just as important to the sustainability of the Foothills' ecosystem as the location of parks and preserves.

For the people moving into the Foothills, it's a point of pride to say that they live "in the woods" or "in the forest." A recent survey of El Dorado County residents, conducted in connection with an update to the local general plan, found that most residents had moved to the county to get away from city life and "live in a rural environment"—even if they continue to commute to Sacramento for work.

New residents tend to want to live on large lots, sometimes five or ten acres. Because local zoning regulations promote the preservation of trees within new subdivisions, the emerging residential landscape does not always look very different from the natural landscape that preceded it. Yet these are the classic conditions of the halo effect. While most of the trees remain, many of the related plant communities are forced out. Roads, especially, cut off essential linkages within the oak-pine woodlands, eliminating crucial wildlife corridors.

The Foothills' ecosystems are fire-driven environments, requiring periodic fires to renew them. And the dry summer conditions of the Foothills make fire more likely in the oak-pine woodlands. In the past, California's wildland fire strategies focused on allowing a fire to run its natural course while safely containing it at the same time. This strategy permitted renewal and also lessened the danger of fires in the near future by removing underbrush and thinning the trees.

When people live in the woods, however, firefighters must take a different approach. They must focus on protecting human lives and homes rather than allowing a fire to run its course. Not only does this approach harm the natural environment in the long run, but in the short run it also increases the risk of more fires in the same vicinity since the flammable underbrush has not been burned off.

These threats to the natural environment have emerged quickly, for the Foothills do not have the long history of conservation efforts that the High Sierras or coastal areas have. Also, there has been no single rallying issue that has focused the attention of both conservationists and local residents on preserving the natural environment. Now, however, the Foothills are finally getting the attention they deserve.

Indian rhubarb in crevices along a rocky stream, Sierra National Forest

Scott Atkinson

Jeff Gnass

Oak sentinels on a grassy hillside overlooking Middle Fork Kaweah River Canyon, Sequoia National Park

Jeff Gnass

Goldfields and lupines bloom beside a vernal stream, Butte County

Recently, the California Department of Forestry and Fire Protection has spent considerable effort documenting both the natural and fire-related threats to the Foothills. For example, the state developed a map showing the likely impact of urban development—meaning development of five-acre lots or denser—on the Foothills counties. It shows an almost total loss of natural communities if local general plans are implemented. This stark picture alarmed even the local residents, who traditionally have not been active in conservation efforts. Now, Foothills counties are working with state officials to examine fire-fighting strategies and the impact of development on the Foothills' oak-pine ecosystem. More recently, major conservation philanthropies have made the Foothills a focus of their preservation efforts.

The Foothills are not, so to speak, out of the woods yet. People will not stop moving to the Foothills from the Bay Area and Southern California; indeed, if current socioeconomic patterns continue, this migration is likely to accelerate. Plus, there is still a great deal of popular support for low-density subdivisions so that people who want to can live "in the woods." It is difficult for the subtle beauty of the Foothills and the oak-pine woodlands to compete for attention with such high-profile scenic wonders as the California coast, the redwood forests, and the High Sierras. Yet the environmental issues facing the Foothills must be addressed.

The Foothills are where the path to California's prosperity began a century and a half ago. They may also be the place where sustainable prosperity—economic stability combined with environmental conservation—must begin in the twenty-first century. If conservation in the future means making difficult choices outside the traditional mainstream of environmental activism—and doing it carefully so that the building blocks of the state's prosperity and quality of life remain strong—then the Foothills are the logical place for this effort to begin.

Fred Hirschmann

*Chaparral whitehorn and
redbud in bloom, Sequoia
National Park*

John Fielder

Oaks silhouetted against a morning sky, Mendocino National Forest

Oak and buckeye woodland, Sequoia National Park

Sheep graze along the east slope of the
Sierra Nevadas

Fred Hirschmann

Larry Ulrich

Slate outcrops, Calaveras County

Larry Ulrich

Valley oaks against a fiery sunset, Sonoma County

Moon high above a boulder field with buckeye trees, near Knights Ferry

The Forest

CHAPTER TEN

Deep in the redwood forest, it's much darker than you'd think. In a place like Headwaters Forest, the virgin stand of redwoods near Fortuna that has become an environmental cause célèbre, the legendary coast redwoods rise some three hundred feet high, monopolizing the sunshine and forcing other, smaller trees to twist and turn in order to capture enough light to survive.

The phrase "primeval forest" is a cliché, but in this case it's true. The redwoods are among the oldest living things on earth. Some of them date back more than two thousand years. In a fire-driven forest ecology, they are remarkably fire-resistant, able to sprout new roots easily and create a ring of clones that protects the parent tree. Simply being in their presence can be a spiritual experience—so reminiscent of the vaulted ceilings of the great cathedrals—that the towering redwood forests are often described as "cathedral groves."

Below the trees, it's almost always damp; even at the height of a dry summer, the moisture content of the soil might be as high as twenty percent. The forest floor may look like a jungle—ferns can grow ten feet high, and hardy hikers say it can take a couple of hours to move forward just a few yards. In other places the ground supports only modest undergrowth, depending on conditions. There is no question that redwood territory is the closest thing California has to a rain forest.

So it shouldn't be surprising that the legendary coast redwoods—the *Sequoia sempervirens*—are at the center of California's most pitched and seemingly irreconcilable conservation conflict. There is something about the redwoods that seems to bring out the intemperate in everyone—the most strident environmentalists, the most vocal lumberjacks, the most aggressive financiers. The conflict over the redwoods has echoed across the television news so often that the species at risk are almost household names—spotted owl, coho salmon, marbled murrelet. Meeting the conservation challenge of the California redwoods will likely require steps that are expensive and politically difficult. And even then, the stridency and the conflict may not cease.

The redwoods are indeed one of nature's most magnificent creations, and they stand at the center of an ecosystem that is important, fragile, and increasingly rare. Redwoods thrive in what might be called the "fog belt" of Central and Northern California—a climate that is rainy in the winter (up to one hundred inches per season in some places), foggy in the summer, and never too

Douglas' lupine and grasses on a hillside, Dolason's Prairie, Redwood National Park

Terry Donnelly

Terry Donnelly

Coast redwoods in Cathedral Grove, Muir Woods National Monument

Larry Ulrich

Western rhododendron beneath coast redwoods, Del Norte Coast Redwoods State Park

John Fielder

Wood sorrel carpeting the forest floor, Humboldt County

hot. The redwoods once ranged up and down the California coast from Oregon almost to Monterey. After a century of harvesting, the remaining stands are centered on the North Coast, especially Humboldt County.

Here, at the epicenter of California's timber industry and its environmental activism, three kinds of forest can be found. First are the reasonably healthy "second-growth" forests that have grown in the wake of clear-cutting. Second are the forests that have been selectively cut—ecologically compromised in some way, but often showing few visible signs of disruption. And, in a few rare instances, virgin forests that have never been touched by a chain saw still exist. These treasured virgin forests still exist in places such as the Headwaters Forest, which is located at the headwaters of both Salmon Creek and the Little South Fork of the Elk River.

The redwood forests stand amid watersheds characterized by steep ravines and short, volatile rivers that run straight to the sea—a characteristic that has made logging difficult from the beginning. Despite their size, the redwoods have a shallow root system, and this makes the whole ecosystem vulnerable. Redwood trees can easily topple over if the soil is wet for long periods of time, and—perhaps important to the ecosystem—their shallow root systems don't provide the soil with much stability. This makes the redwood watersheds especially susceptible to erosion.

California Department of Forestry researchers have found that sediment tends to flow downstream very quickly after a rainstorm, and the biggest sediment flow in a North Coast river typically comes an hour and a half after the peak of the downpour. Cutting the redwood forest only makes the problem worse. These same researchers have found that stream sediment increases 80 percent in areas where roads have been built and 275 percent in areas that have been logged. In a state that has been plagued by erosion problems along the coast for twenty years, the sediment flow is more destructive on the North Coast than anywhere else in California.

Concern over protecting the redwoods dates back almost eighty years, when the Save The Redwoods League first began lobbying for state purchase of land from private lumber companies in what is now Humboldt Redwoods and Grizzly Creek Redwoods State Parks, not far from the virgin stands of Headwaters Forest. More recently, concern over the redwoods—and the redwood ecosystem—has accelerated. Both the spotted owl and the marbled murrelet, a rare bird that nests in redwood trees, have been declared endangered species. So too has the coho salmon, which uses the creeks and rivers of the redwood forest to spawn. The coho's decline has been so precipitous that an estimated population of 500,000 salmon dropped to 5,000 in just two decades—and a $70 million commercial fishing industry completely disappeared.

George Ward

Rhododendron blossoms among western hemlock branches, Lady Bird Johnson Grove, Redwood National Park

Forest trail, Del Norte Coast
Redwoods State Park

Larry Ulrich

Ancient tree trunk, Del Norte Coast Redwoods State Park

Decay and new growth, Jedediah Smith Redwoods State Park

Coast redwoods, Prairie Creek
Redwoods State Park

But further protection of the redwood forest has met with resistance in the lumber towns and sawmills of the North Coast, and also in the boardrooms of San Francisco, Houston, and elsewhere, from which the large lumber companies are controlled.

The North Coast is one of the most remote and least populated areas in all of California. The five counties that make up the North Coast and its watersheds comprise some twelve thousand square miles, or approximately twelve percent of all the land in the state. Yet just one Californian out of every hundred lives there. With no natural harbors and difficult road-building terrain, the redwood empire has always been somewhat inaccessible. The region's remoteness traditionally fostered a somewhat colonial atmosphere, with lumber companies building "company towns" and local residents who had little choice but to work in the timber industry. More than any other part of California, the North Coast has based its economy on a single natural resource. These social and economic conditions are part of the reason why the effort to save the tall trees has been so wrenching.

A vast amount of land on the North Coast is controlled by the U.S. Forest Service. When the listing of the spotted owl as an endangered species forced a change in the way private lumber companies logged on federal land, it touched off heated protests from lumberjacks and others who depended on the timber industry for their livelihood. The most severe conflicts, however, have not been over logging on federal land, but over the fact that the most pristine virgin redwood forests are owned by private lumber companies.

Logging on private land is subject to regulation by the California Department of Forestry and Fire Protection under the state's Forest Practice Act.

Jack Dykinga

Old-growth forest with
sword ferns and redwood sorrel,
Jedediah Smith Redwoods State Park

Such regulation has limited logging in these areas but has not eliminated it. This is part of the reason why the controversy over Headwaters Forest has come to serve as a metaphor for the entire debate over the long-term future of the North Coast forests.

The three-thousand-acre core of Headwaters Forest is a virgin stand of old-growth forest owned by Pacific Lumber Company, one of California's oldest and most respected timber companies. Traditionally, Pacific Lumber had pursued a policy of selectively cutting its old-growth redwood forests and cutting no more board feet each year than could be replaced by natural growth. It was these policies, ironically, that caught the

Coast redwood trunks,
Muir Woods National Monument

Terry Donnelly

Forest canopy,
Montgomery Woods State Reserve

Scott Smith

In the redwood forest,
Myers Flat, Humboldt County

John Fielder

Sunlight penetrating an ancient redwood forest, Montgomery Woods State Reserve

Scott Smith

attention of both environmental activists and outside financiers. By the 1980s, Pacific Lumber held the most environmentally significant redwood groves anywhere on the North Coast—more important than the Forest Service land, which had been heavily logged. But these same old-growth forests also gave Pacific Lumber's landholdings great untapped commercial value, making the company attractive to outside investors.

After a hostile takeover by Houston investors in 1985, Pacific Lumber abandoned its long-standing timber harvest policies and began moving forward with a more aggressive approach. Among other things, Pacific Lumber obtained approval from the state to conduct limited logging on the last virgin groves of old-growth redwoods. Environmental activists quickly mobilized in response. They soon named the grove "Headwaters Forest" and began lobbying for the preservation of a much larger area, consisting of sixty thousand acres—a third of all of Pacific Lumber's landholdings. Caught in the middle were Pacific Lumber's longtime employees, who believed in selective logging but feared that the new ownership would "play out" the forest so quickly that they would soon lose their jobs.

The ensuing battle was probably the most acrimonious conservation dispute in California's recent memory. Eventually, Pacific Lumber's owners came to an agreement to sell 7,500 acres to the state and federal governments (the three-thousand-acre core of Headwaters Forest as well as surrounding land that had only been selectively cut) and to abide by a long-term conservation plan to preserve most of the rest of Pacific Lumber's 200,000-acre holdings.

In many ways, this agreement was a victory for collaborative efforts to further the conservation of natural resources in California. Headwaters Forest's core will pass into public ownership, and most of the rest of the redwood forest will either be protected or logged according to sustainable principles. Yet this agreement has not completely alleviated the conflict.

For one thing, the cost demanded by Pacific Lumber for the 7,500 acres is extremely high—$380 million. This works out to more than $50,000 per acre, a price usually associated with suburban subdivisions, not resource development. At the same time, environmental activists are opposed to the deal because they believe it will not protect the sixty-thousand-acre area around Headwaters Forest that they have identified as significant forest lands. Most North Coast residents, still dependent on the logging industry, remain wary.

Jack Dykinga

Rhododendron blossoms
beneath towering redwoods,
Del Norte Coast
Redwoods State Park

Ron Thomas

Rainforest and ferns, Jedediah Smith Redwoods State Park

Cathedral-like grove of coast redwoods, Del Norte Coast Redwoods State Park

Chain ferns and coast redwoods,
Montgomery Woods State Reserve

They feel caught between corporate interests more interested in profit than timber on the one hand and environmentalists more concerned about protecting natural resources than maintaining the region's economic viability on the other.

While this particular dispute has been going on, the conservation of the North Coast forests has been moving forward in a larger context. The Bureau of Land Management has been actively buying and trading for key properties in the area. Forest Service logging practices have been changed as a result of the spotted owl controversy. Research has provided valuable information about the area's natural systems, especially regarding the effects of erosion and sediment flow. And the economic base of the North Coast has slowly begun to change, focusing more on tourism, education, fisheries, and other more sustainable businesses.

The coast redwoods strike an emotional chord in almost everyone who sees them. The recent battles over how to balance nature and human activity in the redwood forests have highlighted—more starkly than any other situation in California—just how broad-based solutions must be. Twenty-first century conservation in California cannot be the exclusive province of government agencies, environmental activists, investment bankers, or even traditional conservation advocates. They must build common constituencies that can find ways to permit both nature and people to come out ahead.

Douglas irises and horsetail, Redwood National Park

George Ward

Massive coast redwoods, Stout Grove,
Jedediah Smith Redwoods State Park

Terry Donnelly

Sunshine pierces the forest fog, Del Norte Coast Redwoods State Park

CHAPTER ELEVEN

The Valley

Walking across the Valensin Ranch is almost like walking backward in time. Just off Highway 99 between Sacramento and Stockton in the Central Valley, the Valensin Ranch is a noticeable chunk of land, some 4,300 acres adjacent to the Cosumnes River. It's noticeable not just because of its size, but because, alone among the farmlands near the Cosumnes, it was never leveled for agricultural production. It still has all the bumps and undulations that existed all across the Central Valley before the great farming empires emerged in the late nineteenth century. The family that owned the property for 130 years devoted the land to cattle ranching, keeping the natural topography pretty much the way it was.

Of course, the Valensin Ranch is not exactly as it was in 1850. The banks of the creek that flows into the Cosumnes are muddy and mostly bare—a legacy of cattle ranching. The native perennial bunchgrasses have been long since crowded out by European annuals. And Pacific Gas & Electric's huge power lines, complete with concrete pads sunk deep into the pastures, run across the ranch toward the decommissioned Arroyo Seco nuclear power plant only a few miles away.

Still, Valensin has something of the atmosphere of aboriginal California about it. A small pond fills with water in the springtime—a vernal pool. Mallards splash about in this pool, then fly away. Stands of newly planted oak trees, part of an environmental restoration project, show promising growth. The sounds of birds—the killdeer, the meadowlark—are everywhere. And the cows still graze, at least during certain times of year, on certain parts of the ranch.

In its own way, Valensin Ranch reveals a hint of the diverse and vital environment that once stretched along the Central Valley's riparian areas. And as part of the 14,000-acre Cosumnes River Preserve, managed by The Nature Conservancy in conjunction with a dozen government agencies and private partners, the ranch represents an experiment of sorts.

Construction of an agricultural levee along the Feather River around the turn of the century.

Sacred datura beneath a valley oak,
Woodson Bridge State Recreation Area,
in the Sacramento Valley

Herbert Clarke

Wood duck

California Department of Water Resources

The Swainson's hawk, an
endangered species that has
been the focus of conservation
efforts in the farming areas of
Yolo and San Joaquin Counties

The Cosumnes is quite literally the last undammed river of any consequence in the Central Valley. If the Valensin Ranch had not been acquired for conservation, the cows probably would have given way to a subdivision of houses or to the relentless monoculture of grape growing. Now it is being managed with an eye toward bringing back the natural systems still evident along the Cosumnes—but without sacrificing the agricultural tradition of the last century and a half.

The Valensin Ranch and the Cosumnes River Preserve represent one attempt to balance the competing tensions in the Central Valley—tensions that pit nature, agriculture, and urban development against one another every day in every imaginable combination. In many ways, the Central Valley is California's greatest conservation challenge, because it requires a melding of many different economic and ecological interests that are often at odds with one another. The task is made doubly difficult by the fact that, unlike the coast and the mountains, the Valley has almost no base of public land ownership on which to build. Yet the Central Valley also represents California's greatest conservation opportunity—because nowhere else in the state can a large and powerful industry like agriculture be used to help restore the sorely depleted natural systems.

The Valley reaches all the way from Redding in the north to Bakersfield in the south—four hundred miles from top to bottom, formed by the mostly dry mountains of the Coast Ranges to the west and the often snowcapped peaks of the Sierra Nevadas to the east. Encompassing a quarter of the entire state, it includes three large drainage basins—the Sacramento Valley in the north, the San Joaquin drainage in the middle, and to the south, the Tulare Basin, which is often lumped in with the San Joaquin drainage and called the San Joaquin Valley.

These areas form the basis of California's $25-billion-a-year farming industry, the most powerful agricultural economy in the world. The farming empires in the San Joaquin Valley are particularly productive. In 1994, San Joaquin Valley counties occupied six of the top seven spots on the state's list of highest-producing farm counties, and all eight ranked among the top fourteen. The Central Valley represents sixty percent of the state's agricultural productivity and is one of the world's most important breadbaskets.

But today the Central Valley faces not one but two enormous conservation challenges. First, it seeks to retain its impressive agricultural productivity—and its agricultural landscapes—in the face of mounting pressures to urbanize. And at the same time, the Valley seeks to restore many of the natural systems that have been lost—and to do so in ways that co-exist with agriculture, not compete with it.

A century ago, the Central Valley was drained and leveled to make way for cultivated crops. The result was the loss of many irreplaceable resources—especially large mammals, such as the tule elk, which once roamed this expansive plain. And almost all of the region's six million acres of wetlands vanished.

As the vast seasonal wetlands and rich riparian corridors gave way to miles and miles of irrigated crops, much of the region's wildlife adapted to this new environment. Kit foxes were still found here, hunting among the fields and along the creeks and streams. Hawks and other raptors flew above the farms searching for prey. Fairy shrimp still thrived in the vernal pools that remained, or that were created by the new agricultural patterns. The giant garter snake still slithered through the Valley even as heavy cultivation altered the natural ecosystems.

Today all these animals are listed as threatened or endangered species. And like the natural environment that preceded it, the farmland is disappearing. Between 1982 and 1992, according to the federal census of

Jeff Gnass

Sidaleca blooms beside a vernal pool, Vina Plains Nature Conservancy Preserve, Tehama County

California Department of Water Resources

"Fish ladders," such as this one at Nimbus Dam near Folsom, permit salmon and other fish to move upstream without interference

Valley oaks overgrown with vegetation,
Caswell State Park, San Joaquin Valley

Scott Atkinson

agriculture, the state's farmland dropped by some ten percent, from thirty-two million acres to twenty-nine million acres. The number of farms dropped by six percent, from eighty-two thousand to seventy-seven thousand.

The reason is obvious to see: The farms are turning into houses. In fact, all of California's agricultural areas have been losing ground to urbanization for decades. Only two generations ago, Los Angeles and the Silicon Valley were among the most productive agricultural regions in the country. Following this same trend, urbanization is now sweeping through the Central Valley as well.

More than five million people live in the great ellipse from Redding to Bakersfield—almost as many as live in the San Francisco Bay Area. Close to two million have arrived since 1980. Sacramento is now a metropolis of well over one million people. The Valley's "middle counties"—the areas around Stockton, Modesto, and Merced—are inundated by first-time homebuyers from the Bay Area looking for an affordable place to put down roots.

The Fresno area, though still mostly agricultural, is approaching a population of 800,000 people, and Bakersfield is booming too. The sparsely populated northern portion of the Sacramento Valley, a haven for both ranching and farming, has grown by fifty percent in the last twenty years, and the two biggest cities, Redding and Chico, have doubled in size. The state's demographers predict that by the year 2040 the Valley will have twelve million residents—more people than live today in Los Angeles and Orange Counties combined.

The impact of all this urbanization on California agriculture is likely to be grim indeed. The America Farmland Trust estimates that if this growth is allowed to sprawl across the land-scape, perhaps as much as 1 million acres will be lost—along with $2 billion a year in revenue. Some projections estimate that if current growth patterns continue, the Central Valley will be a net importer of food by the year 2050.

Pursuing the aggressive development of agriculture over the years, the Central Valley has not traditionally been the focus of conservation measures. Indeed, until recently few people—even in the Valley itself—truly appreciated the natural wonders that this area originally held. Given the Valley's vastness, its political leaders did not have to con-cern themselves much with preservation of farmland.

Now these traditional views are changing. The Central Valley is no longer overlooked by the rest of the state; rather, it is recognized as a vital and important part of the California narrative. With this increased visibility has come a new understanding that both the Valley's agricultural base and its natural systems are crucial to California's future. In the Valley and elsewhere, there is a recognition that these two vital resources must be preserved together—or else they will not be preserved at all.

The rising tide of concern about the future of the Sacramento–San Joaquin Delta has done much to create this new awareness. The Delta is the ecological epicenter of the Valley, for virtually all of the Valley's water flows toward it. The Delta is also the lifeblood of the agricultural economy, because it is a critical component of the complex system that redistrib-utes water to enhance farm production.

Large mammals such as this elk have become rare since the natural land-scapes of the Central Valley were drained and levelled for agriculture.

Vineyards in Amador County on the edge of the Central Valley. Wine grapes are one of the fastest-growing high-priced specialty crops in California.

Moon over the Sacramento River at sunrise,
Woodson Bridge State Recreation Area

Scott Smith

The current effort to restore the Delta to ecological health will undoubtedly draw some water away from the Valley's farms and it may even take some marginal farmland out of production. The process of making these choices will require both conservationists and agricultural interests to broaden their ways of thinking and work collaboratively.

Elsewhere in the Valley, agricultural interests, conservation groups, and government agencies are engaged in other efforts to revive the region's natural systems, especially riparian areas and wildlife habitats. Farmers from Stockton to Fresno, for example, recently joined with the Natural Resources Defense Council, the Pacific Coast Federation of Fisherman's Associations, and the U.S. Bureau of Reclamation to establish a habitat restoration program along the San Joaquin River and its tributaries. Their goal is to restore riparian corridors, permitting easy movement of wildlife, and to revegetate and stabilize the riverbanks in order to control erosion and reduce sediment flow.

Similarly, other farmers in the Central Valley have been working with their local county governments—and with urban developers as well—to restore riparian habitats. Yolo County's habitat management plan, for example, calls for developers to finance a mitigation program that will restore riparian corridors adjacent to existing farmlands to improve habitat for the endangered Swainson's hawk, among other species. Other counties appear ready to follow suit.

Ross's geese

Herbert Clarke

Given the growth pressure on the Central Valley, any efforts to address either farmland preservation or enhancement of natural systems will necessarily have to deal with the future urban development of the Valley as well. The Valley's once-charming small towns are now sprawling outward with Los Angeles-like aggressiveness across this seemingly endless plain. Such sprawl will serve neither agriculture nor the natural environment well.

Crafting a solution for the Central Valley will not be easy. Yet it is agriculture, which transformed the original landscape in a radical manner, that holds great promise for restoring and enhancing the natural environment. Both future farming practices and urban development must be crafted within the context of restoring natural resources on private lands. This is a most difficult balancing act—which is why the Central Valley may be the ultimate test of California's commitment to conservation.

California Department of Water Resources

Since the invention of the tractor a century ago, large-scale agriculture has been the rule in the Central Valley.

Almond trees in the Central Valley. Fruits and nuts are an important part of California's unusually varied agricultural production.

California Department of Water Resources

Spring grasses and a grove of valley oaks,
Bidwell Park, near Chico

CHAPTER TWELVE

The Coast

There is perhaps no spot anywhere along California's 1,100-mile coastline that reflects the identity of the place and its people more than San Simeon Point. It protrudes into the sea along the jagged Central Coast, just across Highway 1 from the famous Hearst Castle, halfway between Los Angeles and San Francisco. Here, beyond groves of eucalyptus trees and Monterey pines, virtually everything that Californians value about their intense relationship with the ocean lies within easy view.

Look seaward, especially in the spring, and you might catch a glimpse of whales, dolphins, and other sea mammals. Cast your gaze to the north and you'll see the famous stretch of coastal dunes heading toward the Piedras Blancas Lighthouse, where thousands of elephant seals, once hunted to the brink of extinction, come ashore to mate and rest. Immediately below the bluffs on which you're standing lies the magical world where the shore meets surf. Dramatic rock formations, including a rock arch, rise from the waters and tidepools teem with aquatic life.

Onshore, you're surrounded by dozens of colorful wildflowers, many of them found in few other locations along the coast. Even the eucalyptus and Monterey pine groves, apparently planted early in this century by William Randolph Hearst, are alive with color, as they have become an important roost for monarch butterflies. And looking inland, you'll see the spectacular 77,000-acre Hearst Ranch, whose grassy hillsides and grazing lands provide the signature landscape of the Central Coast.

San Simeon Point and the drive along Highway 1 have often been described as the best remaining examples of the old California coast. Today, the area represents both the success that California has achieved in preserving the coast and the challenge that Californians face in maintaining both coastal and ocean resources in the future.

To Californians, the Pacific Ocean has always represented a connection to the outside world as well as a separation from it. The drama of the coastline, with its rugged mountains, rocky bluffs, and sandy beaches, has provided Californians with much of their sense of identity. This special relationship between the people and the coast was permanently bound in 1972, when the voters approved a statewide initiative that created the Coastal Commission. Since that time, development along the coastline has been limited, while public access to the coast—along with public awareness of the importance of coastal resources—has grown dramatically.

Mosaic of beach stones and kelp, near Shell Beach, Sonoma Coast State Beach

George Ward

George Ward

Sunrise-burnished cliffs at Drakes Beach, Point Reyes National Seashore

Fred Hirschmann

Sunshine streaming through a wave-carved sea arch, Julia Pfeiffer Burns State Park

Larry Ulrich

Sandstone concretions on Bowling Ball Beach, Mendocino State Park

Jack Dykinga

Sunset on Big Lagoon, a saltwater marsh along the California Coast

Today, Californians have begun to recognize that there is more to their relationship with the ocean than simply shielding the coast from development and enjoying its spectacular vistas. The coastline is at the center of a complex web of relationships between the land and the sea, an interconnectedness that affects both people and natural systems.

Californians are also beginning to realize the importance of their economic relationship to the coast and the ocean. As is characteristic of California, this prosperity is based on both connection to the outside world and escape from it. The ocean and the coast provide the basis for a $17 billion economy, employing more than 370,000 people. Most of the economic activity comes from tourism and recreation (the escape), and seaports and ship-building (the connection). Other industries, such as commercial fishing and offshore oil drilling, play a smaller but still important role in California's economic link to the sea.

Californians are also coming to understand that their relationship to the ocean is a fragile one. It is a relationship that requires not just an awareness of the environmental and economic realities, but also constant nurturing. The viability of California's coast and ocean depends on how we approach a wide range of human activities on the ocean, along the coast, and even far inland.

California's fisheries are collapsing with dramatic speed, as the story of the Monterey Bay sardine industry is repeating itself up and down the coast. Commercial fishing accounts for about $500 million a year in economic activity for California, which is only about three percent of the state's ocean-related economy. But this relatively low percentage is hardly surprising when you consider that California's commercial catch has dropped by three-quarters since its peak sixty years ago—from 1.8 billion pounds of fish in 1935 to only 425 million pounds in 1995.

For many popular commercial fish—the red sea urchin and Pacific angel shark, for example—drops of seventy to eighty percent just since the 1970s are not uncommon. The collapse of fisheries has been especially alarming in the Santa Barbara Channel, the stretch of water between the Ventura coast and the Channel Islands that has always teemed with aquatic life. Five species of abalone have traditionally been fished in the channel; all are now in serious trouble, and one—the white abalone—is near extinction. Twenty years ago, commercial fishermen typically harvested around 100,000 white abalone a year. Today, the white abalone is rarer even than the California condor; only eleven of these mollusks are known to exist. In 1997, California officials finally shut down abalone fishing in the channel. Abalone numbers had dwindled so much that, as one state official said, they "can't seem to find each other to reproduce."

Even if they are unaware of the ocean's resources, Californians probably view their relationship with the shoreline itself as sacred. Here, after all, is the remarkable territory where two dramatically different forms of nature come together, creating an environment that supports a rich variety of both aquatic and terrestrial life.

Purple sea urchins in a tidepool at low tide, Fitzgerald Marine Reserve, Moss Beach

Scott Atkinson

Coastal headlands and rocky shores,
Montana de Oro State Park

Scott Atkinson

Camel Rock, as seen from Houda Point, Humboldt County

Kathleen Norris Cook

Rolling hills near Morro Bay

Tidal wetlands provide a crucial link between the land and the sea. California's tidal wetlands have distinct characteristics that set them apart from their East Coast counterparts. Though some include thriving vegetation above the mean high tide line, California coastal wetlands are much more likely to consist of mud flats.

Scott Atkinson

Kelp and sea wrack at low tide,
Salt Point State Park

These seemingly unsightly areas look like little more than an expanse of mud that stretches between the high and low tide lines. Yet mud flats contain an impressive array of organisms, and they are extremely fertile areas that can support many of California's native plants. These wetlands serve as an important link for migratory birds traveling the Pacific flyway; one million birds per year use the California wetlands during their annual migrations. Even a small coastal wetland may attract forty or more species of water-related birds. And like wetlands everywhere, California's wetlands filter and purify the water, playing an important role in water quality. They also buffer against erosion and serve as crucial nurseries for commercially important fish species.

Yet California has not treated its 110 coastal wetlands with much respect over the last century and a half. Most wetlands have been eliminated by human activity; the total acreage has dropped from an estimated 381,000 at statehood to 125,000 acres today. Perhaps the most obvious example is San Francisco Bay, where dredging and filling reduced the overall size of the Bay by a third. The most serious eradication of coastal wetlands has been in Southern California, where massive development of ports and cities has left the region with no pristine wetlands.

California's relationship with the coast and the ocean does not begin at the shoreline; it actually begins deep in the state's interior—at the headwaters of rivers and streams. Because these rivers and streams flow to the sea, the way Californians manage human activity in these upland watersheds goes a long way toward determining the ecological health of the ocean and related natural systems along the coast. This, in turn, affects fishing, tourism, and many of the other economic sectors that depend on the ocean.

California has some 7,800 square miles of inland watersheds. Human manipulation of these watersheds, much of it far away from the ocean itself, has created many of the state's most serious coastal problems. In the last twenty years, for example, coastal areas from Santa Cruz to San Diego have suffered from severe erosion problems. During this same period, the ocean's water quality deteriorated, often causing public health problems for swimmers,

Monterey cypress grove on granite cliffs, Point Lobos State Reserve

Island oaks on Soledad Peak, Santa Rosa Island, Channel Islands National Park

Larry Ulrich

San Augustine Beach, part of Hollister Ranch, Santa Barbara County

John Fielder

Evening light, San Mateo County

surfers, and others who regularly use the ocean. Both of these problems can be traced, in part, to human activity upstream in the watersheds.

Stream channelization and the construction of dams have increased sediment runoff and hastened the flow of pollutants into the sea. Often, urban drainage systems have consisted of little more than concrete chutes to the sea. In Santa Monica Bay alone, for example, there are five thousand miles of pipes and sluiceways draining into the Bay from a watershed of only four hundred square miles. The decline of coastal wetlands, and their vital filtering function, has made it difficult for coastal ecosystems to absorb these increased amounts of sediment and pollutants.

The depth and range of conservation challenges along the coast may seem intimidating at first, especially since many Californians believe that they "solved" most of these problems by voting for the Coastal Act in 1972. But if there is one advantage in dealing with environmental threats facing the coast, it is that Californians are emotionally engaged with the coastline and accustomed to thinking about it as a high-priority environmental issue.

More so than most of the state's other natural resources, the California coast has given rise to a large number of organizations dedicated to monitoring and protecting it. Santa Monica BayKeeper has played a vital role in focusing attention on the public health problems of Santa Monica Bay. The Monterey Bay Aquarium and affiliated organizations have educated the public about a wide range of issues associated with the coast and the ocean. Dozens of local land trusts along the coast have protected tens of thousands of acres of environmentally sensitive properties.

These efforts, in turn, have generated public support for government programs to mitigate these environmental threats and restore the health of the coast and ocean. California's coastal areas are pursuing some of the most aggressive wetlands restoration and enhancement projects that have been undertaken anywhere. Many of these programs have been controversial, and it is unclear whether damaged wetlands can be fully restored under any circumstances. But at least California's longstanding involvement with coastal issues has stimulated innovative action.

Perhaps the most promising trend in protecting the health of the coast has been the creation of watershed planning efforts throughout the state. Rather than dealing with specific environmental problems, these watershed groups bring together many different people and organizations to take a comprehensive look at the ecological health of an entire watershed. And rather than being created by bureaucratic muscle, most of these groups sprang up spontaneously in response to local problems, yet they have played an important role in bringing upstream and downstream concerns together—so that farmers, developers, and homeowners in inland areas have an understanding of the role their daily activities play in the health of coastal ecosystems. In many cases, inland and coastal areas have altered their own plans in ways that

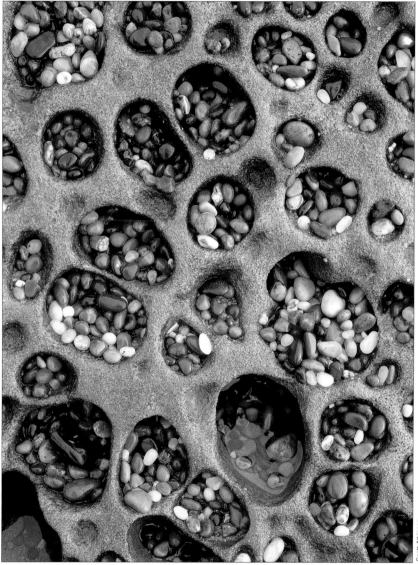

Scott Atkinson

Colorful water-polished pebbles
fill tafoni pockets, near Pescadero

Arch Rock, as seen from Blind Beach,
Sonoma Coast State Beach

Larry Ulrich

Tom Till

Aloe plants in bloom, Laguna Beach

George Ward

Bishop pines silhouetted by a sunset sky, Point Reyes National Seashore

Ron Thomas

Cypress trees in fog, Morro Bay State Park

will help them and help the coast. In Napa County, for example, voters recently raised their own taxes to create a more environmentally friendly flood-control alternative along the Napa River, one that minimizes channelization. This not only helps the people of Napa, but also the San Francisco Bay estuary, and ultimately the ocean itself.

The coast has always played an important role in the California psyche. Over the last half-century, this attachment has permitted California to become a national leader in preserving and enhancing coastal areas. In the future, this special connection may stimulate even more environmental activism—activism that focuses not just on the coast, but also on the fisheries and deep-water ecosystems of the ocean and on the inland watersheds where the relationship between Californians and their sea truly begins.

Douglas fir cones and acorn shells dropped by an acorn woodpecker, Point Reyes National Seashore

George Ward

*Afterglow of sunset silhouetting sea stacks
on Pfeiffer Beach, Monterey County*

Waterfall plunging into a cove,
Julia Pfeiffer Burns State Park,
along the Big Sur Coast

Jeff Gnass

Point Dume, as seen from Pirates Cove,
Point Dume State Beach

CHAPTER THIRTEEN

The Delta

Road maps of the Sacramento–San Joaquin Delta show where the roads go, but they don't convey a true sense of what it's like to travel on them. Most people swoosh along the edge of the Delta on a typical California freeway, catching just the slightest glimpse of this subtle and complex environment of islands and sloughs. But if you leave the freeways, it's a different experience altogether.

To drive on the local roads through the Delta is to follow a narrow, winding path through a landscape unlike any other in California. On one side of the car, especially in the late winter and spring, you're likely to find a swollen river lapping at the tires. This watery world, an important stopover point for migratory birds, is filled with fish and teeming with waterfowl. On the other side, some twenty to forty feet below you, you might see a barn, a farmhouse, and a plowed field—all below sea level, carved out of the rich peat built up over the centuries from the sediment washed into the Delta from the High Sierras and the flatlands of the Central Valley.

Straddling these two views, it's easy to forget that you're not really driving on a road, but along the top of an earthen levee that keeps the swollen river from spilling over into the farm fields, where the river would otherwise naturally flow. While many of the Delta's contradictions are obvious from this vantage point, dozens of others are not.

It's hard to see, for example, that one-quarter of the water flowing through the Delta is diverted southward, against its natural course, for use by farmers in the San Joaquin Valley and urban dwellers in Southern California. It's hard to see the fragile islands that have been sliced in half to make way for the deep-water ship channels that take five million tons of cargo a year to the ports of Sacramento and Stockton. And it's hard to see the central role the Delta plays in the daily life of California—both in the ecological health of the state's natural systems and in everyday human activities.

The Sacramento–San Joaquin Delta is the least characteristic California landscape and also the most important. In a semi-arid region like California, the Delta is a pulsating water-scape that serves quite literally as the pump for California's lifeblood. Each year, some twenty-seven million acre-feet of water flow through it via a series of rivers and sloughs. The water drains off the western slope of the Sierras, and from the rain-soaked mountains of far Northern California, into the Sacramento and San Joaquin Rivers. On its natural course, this water flows toward the greatest estuary on the West Coast, San Francisco Bay.

Grasses and rushes, Cosumnes River Preserve, Sacramento Valley

Scott Atkinson

Scott Atkinson

Trapper Slough, San Joaquin Delta, near Stockton

Suisun Marsh near the Delta. At one time windmills accounted for 40 percent of all energy production in California.

Springtime flooding in the Delta. Farmers have built

some 1,200 miles of levees to try to minimize such flooding.

The Sacramento–San Joaquin Delta is an unusual natural formation, built up over the centuries almost from the inside out. The typical delta—the Nile or the Mississippi—spreads its fertile sediment in coastal areas near the mouth of the river. The Sacramento–San Joaquin Delta formed inland, because the Carquinez Straits near Martinez choke off the flow of sediment to San Francisco Bay. The result is a textbook example of nature's richness and volatility.

Scott Atkinson

Wild grape leaves in fall color, Sacramento Delta

In its natural state, it is hard to differentiate the wet from the dry in the Delta. The sediment buildup created dozens of islands, but many of them lie below sea level and therefore are often flooded during the rainy season. Salt water intrusion is a constant concern in the Delta, having ebbed and flowed throughout California's recorded history, depending on the amount of rainfall and other weather conditions. Because of such volatility, the Delta is a subtle, meandering miracle of nature. Together with the San Francisco Bay, it's part of a larger ecosystem that connects the riparian corridors of the Sierra Nevadas and the Central Valley with the tidal flows of the Pacific Ocean.

All these conditions have created a unique environment in which more than three hundred varieties of plants and animals thrive. The Delta's landscape contains a huge range of water-related natural communities, including riparian forests, tules, bulrushes, reeds, and cattails. These are spectacular settings for all kinds of birds; some use the Delta for migration, while others, such as the greater sandhill crane, winter there. A century and a half ago, grizzly bears roamed the Delta; today many small mammals continue to thrive in the Delta, including muskrats, beavers, and mink.

As nature writer Harold Gilliam once wrote: "If the Delta were almost anywhere but California—in the Midwest, for example—it would no doubt have been heralded as a major scenic wonder and perhaps would be protected as a national park." California, however, had more spectacular natural wonders to worry about in the late nineteenth century, and the Delta became the focus of some of the state's most important human activities. The fertile sediment on the Delta's islands—rich peat piled up to sixty feet high in some cases — was prime raw material for agriculture. Over the past century, farmers built some 1,200 miles of levees to control the Delta's extreme water fluctuations, along with 1,800 different agricultural water diversions, thus creating the foundation for an agricultural industry worth a half-billion dollars a year in the Delta alone.

The Delta's watercourses also provided the potential for deep-ship channels cutting inland toward Stockton and Sacramento; for a recreational wonderland that accommodates more than 80,000 pleasure boats each year; and for the hydraulic miracles of the state's two major water systems, the federally operated Central Valley Project and the State Water Project. Both these projects dam rivers on the western slope of the Sierra and send the water cascading into the Delta according to a schedule suited to the needs of agriculture and cities.

The rich peat of the Sacramento–San Joaquin Delta can be as much as 60 feet deep, creating fertile conditions for irrigated agriculture

*Yellow irises blooming in profusion
in the Sacramento River Delta,
San Joaquin County*

Larry Ulrich

Freshwater slough, marsh grasses, and valley oaks, Delta Meadows, near Locke

California Department of Water Resources

The State Water Project's pumping plant at Tracy. These pumps draw water south across the Delta for delivery to the San Joaquin Valley and Southern California.

Much of the water in the Delta is pumped southward toward its human destination, instead of flowing westward toward its natural destination in the San Francisco Bay.

This human manipulation of the Delta is one of California's most impressive transformations, and in many ways it represents the foundation of the state's modern prosperity. Yet it has also placed great pressure on the Delta's natural systems. The draining of marshes to create agricultural land has significantly altered the network of wetlands that was, historically, heavily used by ducks, geese, swans, and other waterfowl. The pumping systems have disrupted the natural flow of water so severely that a third of the Delta's fish species are listed as endangered or are under special study, including the Delta smelt, longfin smelt, chinook salmon, and American shad.

The Delta smelt—currently listed as a threatened species—is a good example of a fish that has traditionally thrived in the Delta's waters but today struggles to survive. The smelt is a tiny fish, rarely more than three inches long, with a pale bluish-gray color that often appears practically translucent. Unlike chinook salmon, which use the Delta to spawn, the smelt lives in the Delta its entire life. And it rarely lives more than a year, meaning its population is extremely sensitive to environmental disruption. The smelt is susceptible to changes in the flow of water and the salinity level, and it can be easily displaced by foreign species.

While native species like the smelt struggle to survive, foreign species thrive in both the Bay and the Delta, adding to the pressure on natural ecosystems. Marine biologists from the University of California, Berkeley, recently concluded that the Bay-Delta area has been so disrupted by foreign plants and animals that it is now "the most invaded aquatic ecosystem in North America." More than two hundred non-native species have entered the system, ranging from crabs to grasses, and many of them are crowding out the native plants and animals. For example: The Asian clam *Potamocorbula amurensis*—unknown in the Delta as recently as the 1980s—is now being counted at up to two thousand clams per square foot in some parts of the Delta. The clams gobble up most of the food supply, leaving little for native plants and animals.

The natural systems in the Delta are under pressure because the Delta's resources are used to fulfill the needs of all of California. So it's not surprising that restoring the Delta's ecological health will require an effort that involves the whole state.

Over the past few decades, a multitude of government agencies have taken an interest in the future of the Delta. State and federal wildlife agencies became involved when the Delta smelt and other species were declared threatened or endangered. Water agencies throughout the state control the flow of water through the Delta, while at the same time water pollution officials in both Sacramento and Washington have become concerned about the quality of the water supply. More recently, California has established the Delta Protection Commission to manage land use in the five-county Delta area.

All these interests have now converged into one of the largest and most comprehensive conservation efforts ever undertaken. The so-called CALFED initiative has brought together California state officials with federal leaders as well as

Bullock's oriole

Stephen Francis

Black-necked stilts in San Joaquin Marsh

Stephen Frances

landowners, environmental groups, and other interested parties in an attempt to restore the Delta's ecological health while continuing to meet California's water needs.

The bureaucratic details of the CALFED initiative could easily fill a book, but the underlying principles are not hard to grasp. The Delta ecosystem is threatened by the intense human manipulation of the region's water flows, which is guided by decisions about water storage and water usage everywhere from Oroville to San Diego. Because it carries half the water runoff in the state, the Delta is susceptible to minute alterations in water management, especially within the dikes and levees of the Delta itself. Restoring the Delta to health requires a fundamental shift in the way all this water is moved, stored, and used.

As with all large-scale conservation efforts, helping the Delta will require Californians to make a series of difficult choices—and it will require a considerable investment as well. The hydraulic improvements being considered under the CALFED initiative—the new construction required for the Delta to operate more efficiently—is expected to run into the billions of dollars. (Hundreds of millions of dollars in state and federal funds have already been appropriated.) In addition, Californians will probably have to make a controversial decision about whether or not to pump water around the Delta, rather than through it, in order to move it southward more efficiently. And a comprehensive solution to the Delta problem may well call upon Californians to take some valuable farmland in the Central Valley out of production in order to permit more water to flow through the Delta and into San Francisco Bay.

None of these decisions will be easy ones. But making them in a thoughtful and forward-looking way lies at the center of California's success in the twenty-first century. It may be an uncharacteristic landscape for a semi-arid state, but the Sacramento–San Joaquin Delta continues to form the foundation of California's prosperity and its ecological balance.

Courtesy Metropolitan Water District of Southern California

An irrigation canal
in the Delta

Hyacinth blanket Trapper Slough, San Joaquin Delta

CHAPTER FOURTEEN

The Scrub Coast

Up in the hills, it's the aroma that hits you first—the sweet, minty smell of sage wafting across the hillside. Then, after a while, you'll feel the sun. It's desert-harsh in midday, even in winter, yet still tempered by a cool breeze blowing inward from the ocean only a few miles away. And when you begin to look around carefully, you'll notice the wildlife. Red-tailed hawks hovering above, waiting for a snack. Rodents scurrying across the patchy ground below. And small point-beaked songbirds perched in the low, woody branches of the scraggly shrubs that stretch across the landscape.

The shrubs are easy to overlook at first. But except for the hills themselves, they are the dominant feature of this backcountry landscape. Unlike so many other distinctive elements of the California landscape —the redwoods, Yosemite, Death Valley—the shrubs aren't overwhelming or majestic. They're maybe four feet high and spread across the landscape in intermittent patches. Sometimes the shrubs are so spread out that whole other ecosystems lie between them.

And yet, these shrubs form the basis of one of the most important and fragile ecosystems anywhere in California. There are sage and sagebrush and sometimes, especially in dry spots, you'll find prickly pear cactus. This ecosystem supports a startling array of wildlife and constitutes one of the last remaining refuges for small songbirds, including the California gnatcatcher and the cactus wren. Sometimes called soft chaparral, to distinguish it from "real" chaparral, this ecosystem is more often known as coastal sage scrub.

This wild landscape of coastal sage scrub is part of an emerging preserve of nearly forty thousand acres intertwined with some of the most expensive real estate in the world. If you're high enough on any hill in the preserve, you can probably see the ocean. But you'll also see the loose web of freeways, subdivisions, and office buildings

Cactus wren

Stephen Francis

Coastal ridges, near Laguna Beach—lands owned
by The Irvine Company, Orange County

Stephen Francis

with which the gnatcatchers and the cactus wrens must share the part of Orange County that has historically belonged to them.

For more than a century, coastal sage scrub has been a prominent backdrop of the Mediterranean-style urban life in Southern California. But one of the ironies of Southern California as a region is that even as people have been drawn here by the natural environment—the climate, the dramatic vistas, the soothing combination of dry air and tempering ocean breezes—they have eradicated the very things that make it special. And so, over the past hundred years, the sage, the sagebrush, and many other plants have been pulled out in huge quantities to make way for pastures, citrus orchards, towns, subdivisions, and the other accessories of modern life required by a megalopolis of twenty million people.

Lately, however, the urban dwellers of Southern California have begun to appreciate the unusual variety of ecosystems that surround them. The semi-arid climes of Southern California are unique in their biological diversity—and also in the manner in which biology comes face to face with human intervention. Since the arrival of the Spanish some 230 years ago, Southern California's coastal environment has been changed in many ways over the years: cattle ranching, orchards, and subdivisions. Yet, from the mountains to the sea, large areas of land have remained virtually untouched, and a diversity of plant and animal species still remain.

Over time, Southern California's very prosperity has begun to disrupt this balance. Nowhere else in America has modern suburban development burrowed so deeply into such a raw and fragile natural environment. In almost every location where new houses or office buildings are proposed, a spectacular natural landscape is threatened. With the population pressures growing, a major effort is required to maintain these landscapes and the rare diversity of plant and animal species that they support. As University of California wildlife biologist Thomas Scott has pointed out, the script for Southern California's natural history for the next several millennia is being written right now with every housing development, every environmental impact report, and every mitigation measure.

It has not been easy for Southern Californians to come to terms with this reality. From Los Angeles to San Diego, from Santa Barbara to Riverside, the region is accustomed to "having it all"—reaping the benefits of prosperity while retaining a close relationship with nature in an environment of seemingly limitless opportunity. Though Southern Californians have always been outdoors oriented, they have not always been at the center of conservation activism. California's environmental movement has often been focused on the dramatic resources elsewhere in the state: the desert, the mountains, the tall trees.

Over the last decade, however, the pace of change has forced urban Southern Californians to begin coming to terms with the natural environment they have too often overlooked. Their challenge is a daunting one: To carve a huge series of natural preserves—capable of nurturing dozens of rare birds, shrubs, rodents, and other wildlife—out of one of the world's largest urban agglomerations.

The catalyst for this conservation effort has been the plant and animal species, like the California gnatcatcher, that are threatened with extinction. But the Southern California effort has differed from the pitched battles over endangered species elsewhere in the country. The landscapes at risk are not in a rural setting, but,

Coastal sage scrub along Upper Newport Bay

Stephen Francis

rather, lie in close proximity to a large metropolis. And much of the land needed for the preserve is held by private landowners who face the intense economic pressure typical of urban real estate markets.

To avoid the "train wrecks" that have resulted from other endangered species battles around the West, Southern California has adopted a proactive approach. Rather than focus on saving individual species on the brink of extinction, the region has created a series of innovative partnerships designed to restore and preserve tens of thousands of acres of natural land so that whole ecosystems—and the plants and animals that depend on them—can continue to thrive. This effort has required the participation not just of state and federal environmental agencies, but also many private conservation organizations, dozens of cities and counties, and hundreds of private landowners in the region-wide Natural Communities Conservation Planning program (NCCP).

The focal point of this massive conservation effort has been the coastal sage scrub ecosystem, which nurtures dozens of important plants and animals and provides the backbone of the region's natural structure. Biologists estimate that some eighty percent of the region's coastal sage scrub has been disrupted or destroyed for agriculture, ranching, or urban development in the last century. Yet large areas of this vital ecosystem still remain. When the NCCP effort is fully implemented, the region will have eleven different coastal sage scrub preserves—some as large as forty to fifty thousand acres—stretching from San Bernardino south, and west toward the ocean at San Diego. The goal is not just to save a few species already near extinction, but to ensure that most plants and animals in Southern California have so much room to thrive that they will never have to be classified as endangered.

California gnatcatcher

The NCCP process in Southern California has not been an easy one. Even with their combined resources, the state and federal governments do not have enough money to purchase all the land necessary for the eleven preserves. And in an era characterized by enhanced concern for private property rights, it has not been possible to simply prohibit development on all the sensitive land that must be protected.

Many landowners, seeking to maximize the profit from their land, have resisted participation in the program. Local governments have also balked on occasion, fearing that the preserves will drain their own financial resources by removing land from the tax rolls. Even conservation organizations have been critical of the program at times, arguing that it does not go far enough in protecting the landscapes at risk.

Yet, over the last decade, the partnerships established by the NCCP have only grown stronger. And because of unusual constraints that exist in the region, the NCCP partnerships have spawned significant innovations to help preserve landscapes at risk throughout Southern California.

In Riverside County, for example, the Metropolitan Water District of Southern California has played a key role in building a large preserve. Metropolitan, the wholesale water supplier for all of Southern California, has committed itself to sensitive land management practices around two major reservoirs. Metropolitan also purchased a four-square-mile ranch between the reservoirs to provide a vital wildlife corridor. The result: Some ten thousand acres of land dedicated to the county's habitat conservation preserve, thanks to the work of one public agency.

In Orange County, the legacy of California's pattern of large landholdings provided an unusual opportunity for large-scale land conservation in one of the most critical areas for the coastal sage scrub ecosystem. For more than a century, The Irvine Company has owned some 140,000 acres of land—about a third of Orange County. For the last forty years, the company has used its land resources to create the urban development that has provided the basis for the county's current prosperity. Recently, Irvine has committed to maintaining and enhancing more than forty thousand acres of land under its ownership—a commitment that will be critical to establishing a large habitat preserve in both the central and coastal regions of the county.

The preserve is managed in partnership with local, state, and federal government agencies, and with private conservation organizations. Conservation on such a large scale would be impossible without Irvine's substantial landholdings, which create the extensive wildlife corridors required for the survival of numerous species, from rodents and birds to bobcats and mountain lions.

In San Diego County, where many communities and small landowners have been concerned about the economic impact of the county's three preserves, the NCCP partners have adopted a number of particularly innovative approaches. In particular, San Diego has emerged as a national leader in the concept of "conservation banking."

Individual mitigation requirements can often be onerous to small property owners, yet they do not always create the large-scale conservation required to preserve entire ecosystems. By allowing landowners to buy and sell their mitigation requirements, conservation banks permit mitigation to be concentrated on large parcels of land with high conservation value. The most highly publicized conservation bank in San Diego is the Carlsbad Highlands project, managed by the Bank of America, which helped conserve a 265-acre parcel of land that would otherwise have been slated for urban development. Carlsbad Highlands is one of about two dozen conservation banks in the San Diego area.

The preservation of Southern California's "scrub coast" is far from complete. While many of the NCCP partnerships are strong, most of the preserves themselves are not yet permanently in place. And there is no guarantee that the political consensus and financial commitments that have emerged over the last decade will hold for the long run. But national conservation leaders from Interior Secretary Bruce Babbitt on down agree that the Southern California effort is a national model for resolving endangered-species disputes cooperatively, instead of rancorously. Finishing the job will require the ongoing vigilance of the people who live in urban Southern California.

Gabino Canyon, owned by the Santa Margarita Company, southern Orange County

CHAPTER FIFTEEN

The Desert

From the mouth of Titus Canyon, it's possible to look westward across the entire expanse of Death Valley and view the kaleidoscopic variety of the California desert almost at a glance. Titus Canyon is a long, narrow, rugged notch that runs down the Grapevine Mountains from Nevada into California along a vertical drop of more than four thousand feet. Traversing the last few miles is a confining experience, hemmed by tall limestone walls that narrow the gorge to only a few feet in width, nearly blocking the sun from view.

From the bottom of the canyon, all of Death Valley lies ahead. The famous, ever-shifting sand dunes are visible immediately in front of you near Mesquite Flat. But contrary to popular perception, there is far more to Death Valley than sand. A little to the south, you can see the salt flats lying below sea level, which can easily be mistaken from a distance, mirage-like, for a sparkling inland lake. In the spring, the view features a sea of bright yellow desert gold and other vibrant wildflowers. And across the valley, the scene is completed with wrinkly, colorful rocks on the west side, and, above them, the snow atop the peaks of the Panamint Mountains, rising a mile or more above the valley floor.

Barrel cactus, Mojave National Preserve

George Ward

Even at more than one hundred miles in length, Death Valley represents only a small portion of the California desert, which covers an area of more than thirty-nine thousand square miles—almost the size of Ohio—in the southeastern third of the state. The natural diversity so obvious at a glance in Death Valley is characteristic of all the state's arid areas. Edwin Rothfuss, the former superintendent of Death Valley National Park, once wrote that when he first arrived he expected the area to be "hot, dry, flat, sandy, and perhaps boring." Soon after his arrival he realized it was "intensely complex, beautiful, full of life, and with a rich history of man."

For most of the last century and a half, Californians have taken Rothfuss's initial view of the desert as a boring, empty wasteland—a kind of tabula rasa on which they could inscribe whatever dreams of human folly they could invent. More often than not the dreams failed, reinforcing the traditional view of the desert as evil—a view still reflected in dozens of desert place-names that seem designed to repel visitors rather than attract them: Death Valley, Starvation Canyon, Devils Cornfield, Dead Mountains, Horse Bones Canyon, Funeral Range, Arsenic Springs, and Hellhole Canyon.

Even in its apparent emptiness, the California desert clearly held far more than just a few monuments to Hades. Journalist David Darlington has written that California's desert is "an

Terry Donnelly

Mesquite trees on Mesquite Flat Dunes, Death Valley National Park

Water rushing down polished granite in Cougar Canyon, Anza-Borrego Desert State Park

Scott Smith

Wind-rippled dunes,
BLM Cadiz Dunes Wilderness

Jeff Gnass

*Blue yuccas and Joshua trees,
Cima Dome Wilderness in
the Mojave National Preserve*

Jeff Gnass

Winding road through the badlands
of Twenty Mule Team Canyon,
Death Valley National Park

unceasing contradiction … an empty place full of activity, a blank slate brimming with meaning, an overflowing void." Its large spaces are deceptively full of natural life and bustles with activity. It is only recently that Californians have gained a true appreciation of these extraordinary desert landscapes, which perhaps best exemplify the state's remarkable biodiversity.

Though definitions vary and geographic boundaries are hard to nail down, it is generally agreed that California has at least two distinct deserts. The first is the famous Mojave Desert—often known as the "high desert"—which stretches from the northern suburbs of Los Angeles north and east across portions of Kern, Inyo, and San Bernardino Counties to the Nevada state line. (Death Valley is sometimes—though not very accurately—considered part of the Mojave.) The Mojave generally lies at an elevation of at least a thousand feet. For this reason, summers can be intensely hot, and winters bitter cold. And because most of it is still relatively remote, the Mojave contains few centers of population.

Larry Ulrich

Sunrise highlights teddy bear cholla, Joshua Tree National Park in the Mojave Desert

The second is the Colorado Desert—the "low desert"—located farther south. It includes the Palm Springs area, the Imperial Valley farming region, and most of the rest of eastern Riverside County and Imperial County all the way to the Colorado River. The Colorado Desert is generally hotter in the summer than the Mojave and milder in the winter. It is much more accessible to a large population base and much more encroached upon by humanity.

However they are categorized, California's deserts share certain characteristics. Like all deserts, they are extremely arid climates, usually receiving no more than eleven inches of rainfall per year and often much less. Death Valley averages only an inch and a half per year; El Centro, in the Imperial Valley near the Mexican border, gets only three-quarters of an inch. Downpours do occur, often wreaking devastation on the desert environment, but it is not uncommon for these areas to go an entire year or more without experiencing a single drop of rain.

With the dryness comes extreme temperature variations. Summer temperatures can average over 110 degrees, while winter frosts are not uncommon, especially in the Mojave. These temperature extremes can occur not just from one season to the next, but often from one hour to the next. With almost no moisture in the air, temperatures drop dramatically once the sun disappears. Daily variations of thirty to forty degrees are typical, and in some parts of the Mojave swings of eighty degrees are possible in a single twenty-four-hour period.

Jack Dykinga

Badwater, a heavily salted pool, reflecting snow-dusted Telescope Peak, Death Valley National Park

Jack Dykinga

Sunset on Mesquite Flat Dunes, Death Valley National Park

*Ibex Dunes, with Ibex Hills and
Saddle Peak Hills in the distance,
Death Valley National Park*

California's desert areas were not always so hot and dry. As recently as the last Ice Age—ten to fifteen thousand years ago—they were full of water. The floor of Death Valley was flooded. This inland lake, later named Lake Manly, was connected by streams and rivers to a whole network of other lakes in the vicinity. When the Ice Age ended, these waters receded, leaving behind shimmering alkaline dry lakebeds rich with

Fred Hirschmann

Desert velvet blooming in Virgin Spring Canyon, Death Valley National Park

minerals. Today, the only large lake remaining in the California desert is the Salton Sea, a large, shallow, salty body of water located halfway between Palm Springs and the Mexican border. It was created almost a century ago when an accidental canal breach sent water into a natural depression below sea level.

A land of such extremes is not easily survived, but a remarkable number of plants and animals have adapted themselves to do just that. The California desert, in the words of nature writer T. H. Watkins, "does not preclude life, but it demands of it a special effort." While desert wildlife is elusive to the typical observer, it is actually quite abundant and diverse. "The deserts of California," writes the eminent California naturalist Elna Bakker, "are more alive than any comparable regions of the world."

There is, for example, the kangaroo rat, a small rodent perfectly suited for desert life. Like so many desert animals, the kangaroo rat is nocturnal, foraging at night to avoid the daytime heat. It never sweats—in fact, it doesn't even have any sweat glands—and it doesn't need to consume any liquids, getting enough moisture from the foods it eats.

Perhaps the best-known of all of California's desert species is the desert tortoise, whose broad range and endangered status has limited human activity throughout the desert. The desert tortoise looks, as one writer put it, "like a walking table." It's so slow that it's easy to catch, and for decades drivers along Route 66 would stop, pick them up, and haul them all the way back to Chicago. The desert tortoise spends almost all of its time underground, some-times even expanding on holes originally burrowed by kangaroo rats.

Ironically, the desert even supports its own aquatic life—most notably, the pupfish, perhaps the California desert's most distinctive fish. The pupfish thrives in the warm, alkaline waters of the Salton Sea and other lakes—both permanent and temporary—across the desert. They can even survive in mud puddles. The pupfish is exactly the sort of unusual species that the California desert breeds. No other fish could survive in the alkaline desert waters, but the pupfish could not exist anywhere else.

The landscape is filled with equally unusual plant life. The Joshua tree has the basic equipment one expects of a tree—a trunk, branches, leaves—yet it looks so peculiar that is should not be surprising to learn that it is really a yucca, not a tree. The creosote bush, the most common plant in the desert, can survive radioactive fallout and live up to ten thousand years through a novel form of cloning.

Kelso Dunes, with the Providence Mountains in the distance, Mojave National Preserve

Rock formations and boulders at
Jumbo Rocks, Joshua Tree National Park

William Neill

Fred Hirschmann

Desert vegetation growing in the lake bed of former Owens Lake, with the Coso Range in the distance

*Ocotillo and yellow brittlebush
in bloom, Yaqui Meadows,
Anza-Borrego Desert State Park*

Terry Donnelly

Far above the desert's valleys soar the raptors, the large birds of prey, such as eagles and hawks, that scan this seemingly barren landscape for food. The raptors give the desert much of its scenic drama. They too are well adapted to the desert's climatic extremes. When the heat becomes oppressive, the birds simply fly somewhere cooler.

Over the years, the California desert has exerted a peculiar power over humans. From the early explorers on horseback to the auto-oriented migrants of recent decades, many have feared the desert and sought to evade it, or to cross it only at night. Yet others have found its allure irresistible, and it is this continuing attraction that is responsible for today's most significant conservation challenges.

More than a hundred years ago, the lode of rare minerals in the colorful, wrinkled rocks began to attract both individual and corporate miners. The nation's loose mining regulations were part of the appeal. But so, undoubtedly, was the vast emptiness that beckoned in the desert—an emptiness that allowed humans to lose themselves in it and still challenged them to conquer it. The impact of these thousands of miners is everywhere in the desert today. Even amid the vastness, it is hard to find a corner of the region without a dirt or gravel mining road.

Today, this vastness still beckons, but present-day explorers often come equipped with mountain bikes, motorcycles, all-terrain vehicles, and other mechanized means of assault. And while they are not searching for rare minerals to extract for their own profit, these hundreds of thousands of recreationalists still come to the desert in response to the region's seemingly incongruous invitations: to lose one's self in nature and conquer it at the same time. They are in search of the quintessential California experience—the jarring collision with nature. Yet in this particular kind of jarring collision, nature often loses. The environmental impact of an unregulated motorcycle race across the desert, for example, can be devastating. Such races can damage sixty percent or more of the native plant cover. In at least one documented case, a single race destroyed more than 100,000 creosote bushes, many of them undoubtedly thousands of years old.

As urban Southern California has grown to fifteen million people, it has sprawled deeper and deeper into the desert—into the Mojave around Lancaster, Palmdale, and Victorville, and into the Colorado in the reaches beyond Riverside and around Palm Springs. All this growth has placed millions of enthusiastic

Ron Thomas

Claret cup cactus, Granite Mountains,
Mojave National Preserve

Desert paintbrush grows in a rock crevice in Hidden Valley, Joshua Tree National Park

Terry Donnelly

Mount San Jacinto, as seen from Key's View, Joshua Tree National Park

Mound cactus among boulders near Kessler Peak, Mojave National Preserve

Jack Dykinga

Jack Dykinga

Boulder trails across a dry lake bed known as the Racetrack, Death Valley National Park

Jack Dykinga

Desert sunflowers, evening primrose, and sand verbena blooming in profusion, Borrego valley

recreationalists within an easy drive of a weekend in the desert. Accommodating recreationalists while maintaining the desert's ecological integrity is the biggest conservation challenge California's deserts face today.

The federal government owns three-quarters of the California desert, and most of it is administered by the Bureau of Land Management, which is the state's single largest land-management agency. The conflicts here have arisen over how the federal land is used and because pockets of private land are interlaced in a checkerboard-like pattern with federal property.

Much of the federal government's desert land has come under greater protection in recent years. The Desert Protection Act, passed in 1994, created million of acres of new wilderness areas. Both Death Valley and Joshua Tree, which is located in Riverside County, have been upgraded to national parks. Large portions of the desert have been placed under more restrictive mining regulations. The BLM has taken a more aggressive approach toward protecting the desert environment, rather than merely permitting commercial and recreational uses.

But these new restrictions have, if anything, heightened the conflicts over how people should use California's deserts. A wide range of recreationalists compete for limited access to desert areas. There is increased pressure for intensive use of the areas not owned by the federal government—to develop them for urban use, for resorts, or for other facilities such as landfills, which simply reinforces the traditional notion of the desert as a wasteland.

If there's one lesson for California about the desert conservation experience, it's that mere public land ownership isn't enough. To remain healthy, the desert requires many different types of protection, partnerships among various government agencies, and the mediation of seemingly irreconcilable conflicts. Most of all, the desert is a reminder that there are limits to the average Californian's desire for a jarring collision with nature. Once in a while, those collisions have to be managed so that nature comes out ahead.

Beavertail cactus,
Anza-Borrego Desert State Park

The California Legacy

At the outset, this book made the argument that one of the most fundamental aspects of the California attitude is a belief in the power of *transformation*—the ability of Californians to take the raw material they have, manipulate it on a grand scale, and fashion something completely new from it. The result may be a new sport, a trendy cuisine, a slang lingo, a theory of spirituality, or a policy initiative. But whatever it is, this transformation seems unimaginable before conception, improbable during the birthing process, and perfectly logical once it has swept the world.

As much as anything else, it is this belief in transformation that makes Californians who they are. But as we celebrate California's sesquicentennial as a modern society, we must ask ourselves how we as Californians can bring the power of transformation to bear on the challenges we face in dealing with our land and natural resources.

The preceding sections of this book tell compelling stories of change in the way that California's institutions are approaching environmental problems. This change is based on any number of trends that have emerged in the last two or three decades: a better scientific understanding of natural systems, a greater awareness of the relationship between urban life and the natural world, a stronger ability to work together to solve problems. And this change is altering California's landscapes both literally and figuratively.

A generation ago, Californians viewed the Delta as mere plumbing; now we understand it as the lifeblood of our state's natural systems. A generation ago, Californians viewed coastal sage scrub as an annoyance to be hauled to the dump; now we see this ecosystem as the foundation of a miraculous biodiversity that has survived the sprawl of a huge metropolis. A generation ago, we viewed resource protection as the purview of government regulators; now we see it as a collaborative process that must also include landowners, environmental advocates, and local communities.

All this change is remarkable indeed. It has altered the attitudes and actions of the state's once-stuffy conservation agencies and institutions. And it represents, in many ways, a deeper and more lasting commitment to resource conservation than California has ever undertaken before. But it does not, as yet, add up to a transformation. It has not yet translated into the creation of some fundamentally new and different stage in the evolution of California as a region.

Yes, we have learned more about our natural resources. Yes, we are working together. But we are still reactive—still "playing catch up" from the historical, destructive trends of resource development. We still have not quite found that ephemeral mix of ideas, ingenuity, and popular success that marks the arrival of a California-style transformation. Meanwhile, every day we see irreplaceable resources compromised in the name of short-term economic expediency.

It is time to blast through the barriers. It is time to leave behind the tangled web of vested interests and bureaucratic turf wars. It is time to stop thinking that preserving California's land and natural resources is a task somehow separated from the task of building California's economic foundation for the future. It is time, in other words, for every Californian to take a moment to realize that in California we *are* our landscapes, and use that revelation as the foundation for a renewed society in the twenty-first century.

Planning advocates Samuel E. Wood and Alfred Heller gave voice to the connection many Californians feel to their terrain in their famous treatise *California: Going, Going....* Californians, they wrote, intuitively understand that "the greatest asset of their golden state, the very goose that has laid and will lay the golden eggs of their pleasures and profits, is their golden land. This land, our bright land—the charm of its open spaces, the vitality of its soils—is the true economic base of this state, its attraction as a place to live."

Believe it or not, Wood and Heller wrote those words in 1962. If they still ring true today, it's because they still are true today. California's land and its natural resources are not merely a lifestyle amenity or a pleasant diversion. They are the foundation for our very society, and both our remarkably diversified economy and our remarkably diverse culture require them to flourish.

Yet today there is an urgency that did not exist even when Wood and Heller wrote those stirring words. Today California has twice as many people as it had in 1962. Today, countless watersheds and wetlands and forests that were pristine and untouched even then have vanished forever. Today we are thirty-six years closer to killing the golden goose.

If we have not quite figured this out yet—if we have not yet turned the landscape into a transforming idea—it is because the idea hasn't yet captured the imagination of the average Californian. And in today's California—populous, diverse, and so big that it's cumbersome—there can be no real transformation without the widespread engagement of vast numbers of people from different backgrounds, different races and ethnicities, and different parts of the state. California's transformation will not truly occur until every Californian recognizes that our land is the foundation of our society. And for this to happen, it will not be enough for Californians to simply understand this idea. They will have to see it and feel it and smell it in their everyday experience until it becomes a part of them.

But is this really possible? California today is changing fast, and most of these changes would seem to make it more difficult for individuals to become truly engaged with their natural environment. In particular, it would seem difficult for California's emerging population groups to make the connection.

After all, California is by far the most urbanized state in the nation. Four out of every five people live in the vast metropolitan complexes centered around San Francisco Bay and Southern California. These people participate in bustling urban economies and live daily lives that would seem, on the surface, to have little connection with California's land and its natural resources

Just as important, the demographic makeup of California's population is also changing. Already Los Angeles County has become a racial mosaic with no dominant racial or ethnic group; soon California as a whole will have the same composition. Recent immigration has given the economy a far more working-class character and renewed the culture clashes that date back to the backlash against the Chinese during the Gold Rush. Meanwhile, the traditional California conservation constituency remains mostly white and mostly middle-class—out of synch, it would seem, with "the new California."

Yet every Californian has a relationship with nature and the natural landscape. For some, it may be no more than a quick glance at a distant mountain range, or the feeling of the hot desert sun or the cool ocean breeze on their cheeks. But for most Californians—new and old—there's a deeper connection, and it goes back to the California attitude. For a century and a half, Californians of all backgrounds have sought out a close relationship with nature. If, as this book suggests, it has usually been a "jarring collision with nature" in which nature is often the loser, then surely this is better than no collision at all. Transforming California is not a matter of introducing Californians to their landscapes, but of asking them to view those landscapes in a different way—a way that reaffirms those landscapes as a part of their identity as people and as Californians.

In a state that has moved over so much ground with so much velocity for so long, this may seem like a tough trick. But it can be done. California's current landscapes—threatened and preserved—provide us not only with visual images that connect with the public viscera, but also with strong story lines that draw people in and allow them to make those landscapes a part of their identity.

In her famous essay "Notes From A Native Daughter," written in 1967, Joan Didion—perhaps the quintessential California writer—briefly tells the story of Valensin Ranch, the piece of land described earlier in this book as one of the building blocks of the Columnes River Preserve. Didion and her family always had a feel for stories about land—her brother is a real estate executive in Los Angeles—and, having grown up in Sacramento, she was entranced by the century-long sweep of the Valensin story.

In her telling, it is a bittersweet, almost cynical yarn about a family striving in vain to become rich land barons, concluding with an image of a Valensin heir living in a house trailer on the charred site of the once-magnificent ranch house. To her, it is a California story first and foremost, especially because it is a story about the double-edged relationship of Californians to their land, and she fears that such stories will be left behind. "This is a story my generation knows," she writes. "I doubt the next generation will know it, the children of aerospace engineers. Who would tell it to them?"

Now the aerospace engineers have come and gone, and their children have grown up. But the Valensin Ranch is still there, owned now by a conservation group and leased out for environmentally responsible cattle ranching. It doesn't quite exist in the form that the native tribes knew a century and a half ago, nor is it quite the same as Joan Didion remembered it thirty years ago. But it will be available as a story for Californians of the twenty-first century, a way for them to connect to the history of their landscapes, long after the aircraft plants in Los Angeles have been turned into shopping malls and condominiums.

California has always been an evolving story, a hothouse of people and activity and ideas headed in unpredictable directions but always building on each other in order to transform. A century and a half ago, Californians were caught up in the Gold Rush, unlocking the state's natural resources in a unique process that laid the foundation for our modern state. A century ago—with large-scale capitalism already in place—Californians were consumed by the frenzy of resource development, using the wealth of the Gold Rush as the basis for extracting the state's many other natural wonders, such as timber, oil, and fertile farmland. Half a century ago—at California's centennial—the state and its people were hurtling into the suburban era by using the opportunities for industrial wealth and power that the state's resource development, and a war in the Pacific, had provided.

Now it's time to move forward again. Only this time, the task of transformation requires us to have a different attitude about our landscapes. Instead of simply using them for material purposes, we must incorporate them into our souls and into our identities as Californians. We must recognize not only that we are our landscapes, but that in an important way our landscapes are us. They are a reflection of everything California has become in the last century and a half, and a symbol of everything we hope California can be in the millennium ahead.

Yes, we have learned more about our natural resources. Yes, we are working together. But we are still reactive—still "playing catch up" from the historical, destructive trends of resource development. We still have not quite found that ephemeral mix of ideas, ingenuity, and popular success that marks the arrival of a California-style transformation. Meanwhile, every day we see irreplaceable resources compromised in the name of short-term economic expediency.

It is time to blast through the barriers. It is time to leave behind the tangled web of vested interests and bureaucratic turf wars. It is time to stop thinking that preserving California's land and natural resources is a task somehow separated from the task of building California's economic foundation for the future. It is time, in other words, for every Californian to take a moment to realize that in California we *are* our landscapes, and use that revelation as the foundation for a renewed society in the twenty-first century.

Planning advocates Samuel E. Wood and Alfred Heller gave voice to the connection many Californians feel to their terrain in their famous treatise *California: Going, Going....* Californians, they wrote, intuitively understand that "the greatest asset of their golden state, the very goose that has laid and will lay the golden eggs of their pleasures and profits, is their golden land. This land, our bright land—the charm of its open spaces, the vitality of its soils—is the true economic base of this state, its attraction as a place to live."

Believe it or not, Wood and Heller wrote those words in 1962. If they still ring true today, it's because they still are true today. California's land and its natural resources are not merely a lifestyle amenity or a pleasant diversion. They are the foundation for our very society, and both our remarkably diversified economy and our remarkably diverse culture require them to flourish.

Yet today there is an urgency that did not exist even when Wood and Heller wrote those stirring words. Today California has twice as many people as it had in 1962. Today, countless watersheds and wetlands and forests that were pristine and untouched even then have vanished forever. Today we are thirty-six years closer to killing the golden goose.

If we have not quite figured this out yet—if we have not yet turned the landscape into a transforming idea—it is because the idea hasn't yet captured the imagination of the average Californian. And in today's California—populous, diverse, and so big that it's cumbersome—there can be no real transformation without the widespread engagement of vast numbers of people from different backgrounds, different races and ethnicities, and different parts of the state. California's transformation will not truly occur until every Californian recognizes that our land is the foundation of our society. And for this to happen, it will not be enough for Californians to simply understand this idea. They will have to see it and feel it and smell it in their everyday experience until it becomes a part of them.

But is this really possible? California today is changing fast, and most of these changes would seem to make it more difficult for individuals to become truly engaged with their natural environment. In particular, it would seem difficult for California's emerging population groups to make the connection.

After all, California is by far the most urbanized state in the nation. Four out of every five people live in the vast metropolitan complexes centered around San Francisco Bay and Southern California. These people participate in bustling urban economies and live daily lives that would seem, on the surface, to have little connection with California's land and its natural resources

Just as important, the demographic makeup of California's population is also changing. Already Los Angeles County has become a racial mosaic with no dominant racial or ethnic group; soon California as a whole will have the same composition. Recent immigration has given the economy a far more working-class character and renewed the culture clashes that date back to the backlash against the Chinese during the Gold Rush. Meanwhile, the traditional California conservation constituency remains mostly white and mostly middle-class—out of synch, it would seem, with "the new California."